SPECTACULAR
SMALL KITCHENS
Design Ideas for Urban Spaces

E. Ashley Rooney

4880 Lower Valley Road, Atglen, PA 19310 USA

Courtesy of Joe DeMaio.

Library of Congress Cataloging-in-Publication:

Rooney, E. Ashley.
   Spectacular small kitchens : design ideas for urban spaces / by
E. Ashley Rooney.
      p. cm.
   ISBN 0-7643-2110-2 (pbk.)
1. Kitchens. 2. Small rooms—Decoration. 3. Interior
decoration. I. Title.

NK2117.K5R66 2005
747.7'97—dc22

2004029870

Designed by John P. Cheek
Cover design by Bruce Waters
Type set in President/Aldine721 Lt BT

ISBN: 0-7643-2110-2
Printed in China

Photo credits:
Front cover photos clockwise from top left: *Courtesy of Kimball
Derrick, CKD of the Kitchen Design Studio; Courtesy of Tere Bresin
ASID; Courtesy of Phillip Ennis, www.phillip-ennis.com; Courtesy of
David Taylor.*

Back cover photo: *Courtesy of Greenspan Photography.*

Title page photo: *Courtesy of Joe DeMaio.*

Published by Schiffer Publishing Ltd.
4880 Lower Valley Road
Atglen, PA 19310
Phone: (610) 593-1777; Fax: (610) 593-2002
E-mail: Info@schifferbooks.com

For the largest selection of fine reference books on this and
related subjects, please visit our web site at
www.schifferbooks.com
We are always looking for people to write books on new and
related subjects. If you have an idea for a book please
contact us at the above address.

This book may be purchased from the publisher.
Include $3.95 for shipping.
Please try your bookstore first.
You may write for a free catalog.

In Europe, Schiffer books are distributed by
Bushwood Books
6 Marksbury Ave.
Kew Gardens
Surrey TW9 4JF England
Phone: 44 (0) 20 8392-8585; Fax: 44 (0) 20 8392-9876
E-mail: info@bushwoodbooks.co.uk
Free postage in the U.K., Europe; air mail at cost.

Contents

Courtesy of David Taylor.

Acknowledgments

Discovering attractive but small city kitchens is rather like embarking on a treasure hunt. There aren't many. You have to work hard. But when you find one, you marvel that so many appliances, so much counter space, so many sets of dishes, and such quantities of food could fit in such a tiny space.

Peter Lund and I have had a wonderful time seeking out kitchens. We went to shows, to shops, to homes. He did the photography, and I did the writing. We marveled at the creativity of these architects and designers.

Over the Internet or through their work, I met many designers who had fascinating approaches to their work and who have participated in describing some of this art.

Susan Aiello, ASID, president of Interior Design Solutions, has helped to promote interior design as a profession by writing for national publications, appearing on television, and lecturing at museums, professional associations, and schools. She has been a featured speaker on the Queen Elizabeth 2, lecturing on "The English Style – Architecture, Antiques, and Decoration." We have never met, but her knowledge and help have expanded this book greatly.

I had never used a designer until I met Jennifer Rand, who designed my kitchen. She led me to a greater appreciation of designers and in many ways inspired this book. Yael and Dalia Tamari and Will Jameson of Dalia Kitchen Designs of Boston enchanted me with their knowledge and enthusiasm for designing kitchens. They were able to describe how to make a kitchen function the way we dream that it should. They have marvelous kitchens in their showcases and a fount of knowledge at their fingertips. Their insights enrich the book.

Finally, I have to thank Paul Doherty, my own friend and computer guru. Without his help, we would not have all these pictures of great small kitchens.

Courtesy of David Taylor.

Preface

—Will Jameson, Senior Designer
Dalia Kitchen Design

The real joy of small kitchen design is that a small kitchen is a truly intimate space. When designing a small kitchen, I feel my goal is to create a musical jewelry box: a highly functioning room, beautifully proportioned room with exquisite detail.

In terms of functionality, the small urban kitchen is perhaps the most challenging design scenario for any kitchen designer. All design is full of compromise: for example, as counter space increases, so storage decreases. The small urban kitchen amplifies this issue. Creating good flow patterns is also a difficult problem to solve in these typically tight and unyielding spaces.

Perhaps the answers to these questions of functionality lie in the true understanding of the client needs. Getting inside a client's head and extracting the real needs and wants are the key to design success. Once these criteria are down on paper, they can be prioritized and tackled in appropriate order. Only then can the layout of the cabinetry be executed.

It is now that the designer needs to use all the smart storage solutions he or she knows. Clever use of shallow wall pantries for dried and canned goods and "magic corners" that have replaced lazy Susan's save space and eliminate "dead zones." Appliance garages can keep counters free from clutter but allow heavy appliances to be close at hand when needed.

Appliances are the workhorses of the kitchen. A designer's awareness of new technologies and products in the kitchen appliance field is invaluable. For instance, new ovens continually clean their heated air by passing it through a catalytic converter. The re-circulated air in the kitchen remains odorless, and no messy, high-heat self cleaning is required – both qualities are particularly useful in a small space.

Once the functionality has been addressed, the aesthetic considerations need attention. In a small space, detail is closer to the eye and therefore maximized in importance. Hardware, finishes, and material choices are paramount, so building this palette is key to success. As always, design compromise is evident at this stage. Balancing the desires of the interior architecture and the client's taste is a tightrope the designer must walk, and a good design is one that pleases both.

In this book, E. Ashley Rooney has done an amazing job in exploring these challenges and illustrated that there are as many varied design solutions as there are spaces to design.

Foreword

Designing Small Kitchens in Large Cities

Exciting Opportunities and Demanding Challenges
—Susan Aiello, ASID, CID
Interior Design Solutions

When it comes to their kitchens, urban clients often have particular needs that present exciting opportunities for kitchen designers, while at the same time presenting very demanding challenges.

Large urban areas can attract the best and the brightest, the most competitive, and the most style-conscious types of people. New York City, for example, probably has more "Type A" personalities, block for block, than many of the more "laid back," smaller cities in rural America. Although such individuals can be quite demanding, they often know what they want, from devouring design magazines like *Architectural Digest*. They understand and appreciate the value of good design and are willing to pay for quality appliances and finishes. They want to lead, rather than follow, so they are willing and often eager to be the first to try something stylish and, perhaps, even cutting-edge. This presents a wonderful opportunity for talented kitchen designers to really show what they can do – to really be creative.

City clients often want something special and prefer designs that are tailor-made to suit their lifestyles as well as the architecture of their homes. A successful kitchen design must not only address a wide range of functional requirements and constraints and harmonize with the design of the rest of the home, but it must also reflect an individual client's personality, preferences, and lifestyle. In a big city, people tend to work hard and play hard, and they want their environments to reflect that. Few truly competitive people want to keep up with the Joneses – they want to leave the Joneses in the dust.

The large concentration of sophisticated and demanding clientele in big cities and the large number of talented and knowledgeable designers foster showrooms that feature the most beautiful, luxurious, and exotic products obtainable from around the world. Since there are enough people who are willing to pay for the very best, the most talented (and often the most expensive) craftspeople can be found in big cities. Such craftspeople enable designers to execute their designs in the best possible manner.

Designing a kitchen in a major city is both exciting and fascinating because of the constant challenges. Often a limitation that at first seems insurmountable will lead to the most creative and interesting designs. My motto is "If you are given a bunch of lemons, make lemonade."

A significant challenge that tests the creativity of anyone designing a kitchen in a major city is lack of space. On the other hand, their small size and the limited linear footage of cabinetry and counter space that they incorporate mean that top-grade materials can be used without the same budgetary impact as the same choices would have on a larger, suburban kitchen. Designers need sufficient expertise in space planning to maximize the effectiveness of every inch of space.

Kitchen design is always a balancing act between needs and wants, but in a major city, it's more like a three-ring circus. In more than twenty years as a professional interior designer doing kitchen construction in New York, I can honestly say that there is never been a dull moment.

Although many of the pre-war apartments in which I work are spacious by city standards, the original kitchens are often claustrophobic, dingy, and badly lit. There is a reason for this. Until World War II, city kitchens did not need to be comfortable, attractive, or well lit because most people who lived in these gracious apartments had live-in maids. Consequently, they rarely entered, much less tried to prepare a meal in, their kitchens. And certainly it would never have occurred to the original occupants of these apartments to actually eat in their kitchens. Today, many urban couples work, and both want to be able to grab a quick bite in the kitchen before dashing off to their offices.

One way of dealing with a lack of space is "borrowing" it from an adjacent room, as I did for the kitchen in an apartment on Central Park West in Manhattan.

By removing the wall between the original kitchen and the maid's room, I was able to design a convenient and elegant room suited to the needs and desires of a modern-day family. The center island can be used for preparing food or for enjoying a casual meal or snack.

Before the space was borrowed.
Courtesy of Jozef Koppelman.

After. *Courtesy of Jozef Koppelman.*

The seemingly spacious new kitchen. *Courtesy of Paul Whicheloe.*

The challenge of too little space is exacerbated by the fact that many city dwellers view all of today's technological innovations that save food preparation and cleanup time as absolutely essential and on their "must have" list, but these items take up precious space. Although professional designers recognize that efficiency is an important criterion in kitchen design, as in all other aspects of their clients' fast-paced lives, they know that the best appliances in the world cannot make a kitchen comfortable and efficient unless there is adequate counter space and storage. Being able to help clients prioritize their requirements, to retain all of their "must haves," and edit the items in the "nice, but I could live without it" category is probably a more important skill for designers in a large city than for their counterparts living elsewhere in the country.

Sometimes urban kitchens are so tiny that it's a challenge to just find room for the basics. The smallest kitchen that I ever designed was a mere 8' x 5', and my bachelor client really wanted a dishwasher. I solved the problem by thinking vertically. The unusual use of a full-depth cabinet over the refrigerator provided storage for pots and pans, and the drawers for flatware and utensils were installed immediately beneath the doors of the upper cabinets. The design capitalized on the height of my client, who at 6' 5" would not have any problems reaching for things on high shelves! Mirrored backsplashes, simple white cabinets, and a honey-colored wood floor make this tiny kitchen look more spacious.

Anyone who lives in a major city such as New York can eat very well without ever cooking. Dining out and comparing notes is a favorite pastime. The sophisticated palates produced by regularly dining on food from all over the world and the ease of purchasing the ingredients to replicate some of the dishes at home create its own challenges. When my clients use their kitchens, they want to create something very special. Why bother cooking if you can't produce something fabulous?

Because urban clients tend to concentrate on exotic meals that will provide an outlet for their creativity and impress their friends, they often own a great deal of specialized cookware. All of this equipment can take up a lot of space. The key to meeting this particular challenge is to find out how often each piece of equipment is used. I once designed a kitchen for a client who said that she owned three fish poachers and sometimes used them all at once. Once I determined that she only poached fish once or twice a year, I convinced her to store the fish poachers, as well as several other large items that she had not used recently, in a closet elsewhere in the apartment.

One challenge that urban designers face that their counterparts in small towns do not is the immediate proximity of neighbors. Because apartment dwellers have people living above, below, or adjacent to the areas that are being renovated, special care needs to be taken to ensure that the construction does not adversely impact their neighbors. When the kitchen is in an apartment building rather than in a private house, the design has to meet stringent code requirements determined by local regulatory agencies and be approved by the architect retained for that purpose by the building's management. Moreover, all work must be done according to building rules and regulations.

Construction projects take longer and cost more in an apartment building because of logistic challenges, such as limited hours during which construction can be done, site protection requirements, noise concerns, elevator access, and parking limitations. In buildings that have been designated landmarks, seemingly simple changes like replacing an unattractive window can be very complex and sometimes impossible.

Often, pipes, vents, and structural columns can get in the way of an efficient room layout. Because these risers and structural elements are shared with other people, they normally cannot be moved. Every challenge presents an opportunity to be creative. Because plumbing risers in the wall made it impossible to create a single large room, I turned one section into a separate butler's pantry, including a bar sink and automatic ice maker, which makes it easy for two people to work without getting in each other's way.

Urban designers and contractors have to be able to work very quickly and efficiently. If a construction project in a private house takes much longer than anticipated, only the owners are inconvenienced. In New York, an increasing number of apartment buildings impose fines for every day that a renovation project runs over schedule, and some of the more restrictive buildings actually stop construction projects that are not completed in a timely fashion. The fact that a homeowner cannot begin construction until the board of the cooperative or condominium gives its approval means that there is always a delay between the completion of plans and specifications and the beginning of construction. And just to make it interesting, some New York buildings will allow construction only during certain months of the year.

Therefore, when undertaking a renovation project in an apartment building, the client must make as many decisions as possible and make allowances for items that have long lead times before the project gets underway. Everyone involved in the project should have a clear idea of exactly what needs to be done from beginning to end. A complete and accurate set of plans and specifications prepared by a skilled designer is worth its weight in diamonds.

Because of all of the extra technical and procedural challenges involved in renovating a kitchen in a large city, it is best to work with a qualified design professional. There are three types of design professionals that one can use: interior designers, kitchen designers, and architects. One way to evaluate a designer's technical competence is to find out if he or she is actually certified to practice the profession. Certified Kitchen Designers, NCIDQ Certified Interior Designers, and Registered Architects have all passed stringent, nationally administered tests that represent tangible proof of technical expertise relevant to the renovation process. A designer's personal experience in working in the city in which the kitchen is to be created is a definite plus. In addition to different local building codes, each city (and to a lesser degree, each building) has its own rules governing construction hours and methodologies.

A good designer will first attempt to understand the way the client wishes to use the kitchen, clarifying both pragmatic considerations (such as how often and how extensively the client cooks) and more artistic matters related to the client's lifestyle and personality. The designer will then use his or her creativity, expertise, and experience to give the client a kitchen that makes the best use of space to meet the client's requirements and that reflects the client's stylistic preferences. These things are true in small towns as well as in large cities. One of the primary advantages of working with a seasoned design professional on a construction project in a major city, however, is that the designer will help the client solve the design challenges presented by big city living and keep the client out of trouble!

Introduction

Many of us, whether we work outside our homes or not, spend a great part of our lives in the kitchen, especially if we love food or wine, arrange flowers, entertain, have young children, care for our pets, eat…

The kitchen is the center of our life at home. It is the heart of our heart.

The success of the kitchen design can have such an impact on the happiness of the household that we should consider our needs carefully. Homeowners often think of kitchen design as choosing new counters or selecting appropriate cabinets. It's a fun topic, but that's only the aesthetics of kitchen design.

We also have to think about the function of the individual areas.

If we have a simple box – like a room with at least one door and one window and good space, we can usually devise a workable kitchen plan. But many kitchens are not that simple. They may have too many doors, windows, radiators, or a fireplace. Their walls may be irregular or a column may intrude. Ergonomic dimensions and efficient, logical, workable working areas become impossible dreams.

The problems multiply in the small urban kitchen. There's all too little space, and every inch of it has to work. If a cabinet opens the wrong way, a pipe is present, or an electrical outlet is missing, the problem is magnified.

In the urban environment, the small kitchen may be one of several small rooms. It may open directly into the main living quarters. Whatever is going on in the kitchen may affect the rest of the home.

And let's be honest: that aroma of onions is far from romantic at 11PM.

As Dalia Tamari of Dalia Kitchen Design points out, "To make a great kitchen, you don't start with the cabinets and the appliances. You start at the beginning: with the house itself, the total living area, and the location of the kitchen within it." She goes on to say, "In our view, the effort of preparing a meal begins outside the house, the moment you begin lifting the bags and carrying the ingredients."

The standard kitchen design concept is the triangle: an efficient path between the three major work areas: stove, refrigerator, and sink. This concept made sense for previous generations, but we do not use kitchens in the same way today. Homeowners are often stressed and trying to make a meal in a hurry.

To design a kitchen to meet these needs, we first need to focus on the activities that occur in the kitchen: the cooking, food preparation, food storage, and clean up. Typical work centers include: food prep (refrigerator and counter space for chopping and mixing), cooking station (range or cooktop and a separate oven), food storage, and cleanup (e.g., sink, disposal, and dishwasher).

A small kitchen forces compromise. If you want more storage, you have to sacrifice that precious counter space. Or perhaps you give up that coveted trash compactor. The details and their relationships become important.

Kitchen designers can help. They offer experience. They are accustomed to thinking about how people relate to spaces, how they work in spaces, and how to utilize a small space to its absolute maximum. They understand how to bend the "rules" and have the creativity to make your room workable. They know about the new devices, appliances, and technology.

In this book, you will see how many designers tackled the problem of the small urban kitchen. You will see how they circumnavigate the problems inherent in the area and how they get creative with ingenious space-saving arrangements, using every cubic inch or foot. Doorknobs and handles may be absent, drawers may be lipped, cupboard doors may slide sideways, and corners may be rounded.

You will also see some kitchens designed by homeowners and review a diary of a kitchen renovation.

We may spend approximately fifty hours a week asleep and more than forty hours a week on the job, but the rest of the time, we are probably in the kitchen. A 2002 survey by the National Kitchen and Bath Association found that kitchens are becoming the "nucleus of the home, functioning as the gathering place for the family…"

Because kitchens are where we gather, they wear out faster than other rooms. Consequently, they are the most frequently remodeled room in the house.

When you go to sell, kitchens are where the buyer looks first to determine whether a home has been well cared for. Nationally, a seller can expect to recoup a good deal of the cost of a major kitchen remodel.

The question is how to do it right – for you. Hopefully, this book will help you design the right kitchen for your way of life.

Good recycling storage can simplify life. The lower level has a five-way separation system for paper, packaging, bio waste, bottles, and tins. The inner drawer provides useful space for storing cleaning materials. *Courtesy of Alno USA, www.alno.com, tel: 617-482-2566.*

A big trend in storage is the use of drawers for storage of bulky items like pots and pans. Here, in a small kitchen, even the kick plate is used. *Courtesy of Alno USA, www.alno.com, tel: 617-482-2566.*

A renaissance in kitchen design has led to storage that is more efficient and practical. No longer do things get lost in the dark recesses of a cupboard. This "magic corner" has a combination of swing and pull-out mechanisms that ensure access to everything stored. *Courtesy of Alno USA, www.alno.com, tel: 617-482-2566.*

Professionally Designed City Kitchens

Pre-War Kitchen

A spacious apartment in a World War II building on Central Park West in Manhattan had a cramped, dark, and uncomfortable kitchen. Fortunately, the client no longer needed an adjoining maid's room. Susan Aiello of Interior Design Solutions combined this room with the kitchen to create a spacious cooking and informal dining area designed to blend seamlessly with the rest of the apartment. She then created a separate laundry room near the service entrance, enhancing the proportions of the new kitchen, while providing a separate utility area that is convenient to the kitchen but is visually inconspicuous.

The original kitchen is long and narrow. *Courtesy of Jozef Koppelman.*

It needs some help. *Courtesy of Jozef Koppelman.*

The renovated kitchen is now light and bright. Artificial light comes from a number of sources, including recessed lighting in the ceiling and the range hood, under-cabinet lights, and light strips inside of the glass-fronted cabinets. A glass-paned door with shirred fabric behind it maintains visual separation between the laundry room and kitchen, while providing additional light and a sense of space in each area. Natural light comes in through the window over the sink in the area that was originally the maid's room. *Courtesy of Jozef Koppelman.*

The white flat-panel cabinets, black and white tile floors, and black granite countertops with a double ogee edge are classic and timeless. Glass-fronted cabinets in the area of the butler's pantry and between the refrigerator and wall oven display fine china and glassware, while wood-fronted upper cabinets near the cook top conceal less attractive items, such as canned goods, boxes, and bottles. The extra-wide drawers in the center of the refrigerator wall are perfect for linens and large platters. Plug molding (which is connected to a ground fault indicator circuit breaker for safety) beneath the upper cabinets provides ample electric outlets, without disturbing the elegant expanse of the full-height granite backsplashes. *Courtesy of Jozef Koppelman.*

One end of the kitchen serves as a butler's pantry and features a bar sink, an icemaker, and an oversized custom wine rack. *Courtesy of Jozef Koppelman.*

The central island does double duty as an informal eating area and a large and convenient surface for food preparation. The lower cabinets between the cook top and the sink conceal ventilation to remove cooking odors, and the integrated flowerbox above the sink conceals the opening for the exhaust.

The custom-designed upholstered seating by the central island and the Roman shade over the kitchen window provide lively splashes of accent color. *Courtesy of Jozef Koppelman.*

Cow Hollow Edwardian

Altos Design's Valerie Lasker lives in a 1920s' Edwardian home in the Cow Hollow neighborhood of San Francisco. The house is on a narrow city lot, only 26' wide, and is one of a row of four similar houses. Like most city kitchens, her kitchen is modest in size – the kitchen area is 11.5' x 16' – and too small for an island. She did not want to encroach upon the adjoining breakfast area or sitting room. Lasker's goal was to create a beautiful, functional kitchen in the existing space with a style that was in keeping with the character of the house.

White-painted cabinets, crown molding, and hardwood floors throughout the room duplicate the period details in the formal rooms. The lower cabinets have especially crafted S-shaped feet. The 30" gas range under a 36" hood, a built-in microwave oven, and a warming drawer are professional-style appliances, scaled to fit the space. The peninsula contains a large, deep, single-bowl sink plus the dishwasher. *Courtesy of Altos Design, Inc.*

This view of the kitchen from the breakfast area shows the new French doors leading to the deck and backyard. The small window overlooking the neighbor's backyard has a sandblasted glass pane for privacy. *Courtesy of Altos Design, Inc.*

In the breakfast and sitting areas, the sofa repeats the color of the pendants, and the custom throw pillows echo the granite and backsplash. The owner's cat is sunning herself just outside the window in the garden. *Courtesy of Altos Design, Inc.*

This view from the same angle shows the wall of cabinetry containing the pantry, built-in refrigerator, and countertop landing area. The placement of the refrigerator, sink, and range creates an efficient work triangle. *Courtesy of Altos Design, Inc.*

The oak barley-twist table and chairs are the same vintage as the house. The short distance from the table to the peninsula makes clean-up easy. The cutout in the wall at the back of the peninsula contains a small touch-latch cabinet with an electric outlet for the "dust-buster." *Courtesy of Altos Design, Inc.*

The pendants over the peninsula and the pewter accents in the backsplash and hardware add interest to the room. *Courtesy of Altos Design, Inc.*

The built-in cabinet with glass doors on the back wall pre-dates the remodel. The sandblasted glass door on the side opens to a light well with stairs to the lower level. *Courtesy of Altos Design, Inc.*

Larger Than Reality

By using a light monochromatic color scheme, glazed-glass front cabinets, and incorporating numerous vertical elements, Darnel Aucoin made this kitchen appear to be much larger than its footprint. The kitchen boasts all current amenities that have been properly scaled to the well-designed floor plan. The center island with heavy, small-scaled seating is just another added bonus for comfort and function. Lots of overhead and task lighting keeps the small space well lit for maximum use while cooking and can be adjusted when entertaining. The kitchen contains lots of visual interest by using a decorative tile backsplash, onlays and corbels on cabinetry, decorative egg and dart crown molding, and colorful accessories.

Entering the kitchen from the breakfast area, you immediately notice the light glazed cabinets and 20" x 20" porcelain glazed tile, which has been installed on the diagonal to enlarge the space. The tile does not have much contrast and blends nicely with the cabinets, so as to keep the eye moving up. It is imperative, to make a space look larger, that most horizontal elements such as flooring and ceiling be kept in the same tones, especially here with a ceiling height of just 7 1/2'. *Courtesy of Joseph Bergeron.*

This closer view shows an open door into the formal dining room, which uses the same cream, gold, and taupe tones as the kitchen. The doors and ash wood doorframes are in a dark stain, which allows the kitchen to flow into both the dining and breakfast areas while adding warmth to the otherwise monochromatic color scheme. *Courtesy of Joseph Bergeron.*

This view gives a better visual of the floor plan that includes an island, measuring 32" deep x 4' long, which houses drawers on the opposite side. Hand-carved acanthus leaf corbels accentuate the island counter, which is 3 millimeter thick Uba Tuba granite with beveled edges. The only dark horizontal element, this grounds the cabinets and adds visual interest. The custom hand-painted light pendent fixture above the island is in the same tones as the cabinets. Rather than being a focused object, it is a vertical element that blends. *Courtesy of Joseph Bergeron.*

This view shows the stacked 30" stainless steel ovens, microwave oven, regular/convection oven, and warming drawer, all neatly placed with enough counter space close by. It also gives a better view of the backsplash, which is a cream-colored, crackled finish brick tile, accentuated with an acanthus leaf border. Natural grass shades in beige and cream tones emit filtered light and blend nicely with the cabinets. *Courtesy of Joseph Bergeron.*

The 36" six-burner professional range adds yet another function to the kitchen. The stainless steel hood, which houses halogen lighting and variable speed venting, is nestled comfortably under a wood panel adorned with a hand-carved acanthus leaf. Storage for spices and condiments is above and for pots and pans below. This view clearly shows the amount of gold quartz that is in the granite, which accentuates the glazed cabinets. A decorative backsplash panel, using the same brick tiles (but turning them on a horizontal plane and surrounding with a handrail), adds visual interest. *Courtesy of Joseph Bergeron.*

Turning to the left, the view is of the side by side, built-in refrigerator/freezer, the large pantry area with double sliding doors, and, at the far end, a hidden utility sink for convenient clean up. This 6 1/2' wide x 16' long area continues the same color scheme. This footprint is a perfect example of "form follows function." As you enter the kitchen with groceries, you can store the cold items in the refrigerator/freezer and place the canned goods and other food staples in the pantry – all in very close proximity. This view also captures a peek into the breakfast area, which proves that you can mix light glazed cabinets with rich dark stained woods as long as everything is kept consistent. *Courtesy of Joseph Bergeron.*

French Country Kitchen

Paul Engemann, Allied ASID, and Suzanne Barnes, Allied ASID, of Austin-Go-Bostin Interior Designs created this kitchen in a small vacation townhouse in Provo, Utah. The owner, a television celebrity, wanted the feel of a French country kitchen. The designers' concept was to give the appointments a collected look, as if the furnishings and fittings had been gathered over time.

The walls are hand troweled plaster, and the floor is 18th century reclaimed terra cotta from the south of France. The chairs below the sconces are Jacobean with their original needlework covers. The French doors leading to the courtyard are draped in antique French toile fabric to which the designers added a coordinating plaid to extend the width of the panels. *Courtesy of Grant Heaton.*

The owners commissioned custom cabinetry and designed each piece with a different cornice or bonnet. *Courtesy of Grant Heaton.*

Wheat and harvest-themed motifs were the inspiration for the decorative carvings. *Courtesy of Eric Markey.*

A Pierre Frey fabric inspired the motif on this hood. *Courtesy of Eric Markey.*

The designers requested that every piece be stained a different tone to help achieve the ultimate goal of making it appear as if each unit of the cabinetry was an antique, installed separately. *Courtesy of Eric Markey.*

The casings in the room are finished in a sage green, cracked over a reddish-brown base. For drama, Austin-Go-Bostin Interior Designs placed a painted, wrought iron architectural detail over the door. *Courtesy of Eric Markey.*

All of the cabinetry was hand-carved in solid alder and finished with a hand wax. Even the interiors of the cabinets and drawers are solid hardwood. *Courtesy of Eric Markey.*

The owners were anxious that their beautiful view of the mountains not be obstructed at the kitchen window. As a solution, Austin-Go-Bostin Interior Designs had trompe l'oile leaves painted around two lengths of the window and installed antique painted metal leaves and pears over the trompe l'oile. *Courtesy of Eric Markey.*

Upper East Side

Manhattan's kitchen spaces are almost always small with little storage space. In this kitchen, the existing cabinets didn't meet the ceiling, creating an underutilized space at the top of the cabinets. The client requested assistance from Victoria Benatar.

To create more storage space and a cleaner look, Victoria Benatar added a 12" laminated piece along the top cabinet following the previous modulation to raise the storage space to the ceiling. She reused the existing interior laminated cabinets, re-facing them with new, full height matte maple doors on the top cabinets as well as new maple drawers, doors, and base at the bottom. *Courtesy of David Taylor.*

The gray tiled floor remained, and the walls were painted with a high gloss decorator's white paint to obtain different reflections and contrast between all the materials and finishes. *Courtesy of David Taylor.*

A stainless steel countertop with a 5" built-in backsplash replaced the former laminated countertop. Other stainless steel details added included a small shelf by the windowsill, the radiator cover, pull handles, and a vintage light fixture on the ceiling. The appliances are all new, including the Sub-Zero refrigerator installed in an existing niche and covered with custom made maple paneling to match the rest of the space. *Courtesy of David Taylor.*

The Open Kitchen –
Living Room Integration

Victoria Benatar renovated this kitchen on the Upper West Side in New York City.

Benatar eliminated the partition wall that separated the kitchen from the living room to create an island in its place. *Courtesy of David Taylor.*

Victoria Benatar installed new stainless steel appliances along with the gray honed stone countertop. She combined birch wood cabinets (from Ikea) with a stainless steel and glass cabinet to create a dialogue between the different materials used and the living spaces. *Courtesy of David Taylor.*

This small intervention integrates the kitchen with the living room as well as generates seating spaces with stools. It also exposes all the apartment windows, illuminating the entire area. *Courtesy of David Taylor.*

High Gloss in the City

Victoria Benatar provided this small New York City kitchen with new high gloss laminated cabinets, black appliances, and black granite countertops. She also opened it up to the living spaces.

She extended a cantilever top to the outside, creating another seating area for the family. She utilized the remaining spaces as niches for wine storage and lighting or organized storage for kitchen accessories such as the blender. *Courtesy of David Taylor.*

By adding new high gloss laminated cabinets from Poggenphol, new black appliances, and black granite countertops, Benatar created a beautiful and elegant contrast that can be seen from the living and dining room. *Courtesy of David Taylor.*

To maintain the clean look, the cabinets do not have pulls except for ones above the microwave hood and the refrigerator. She provided the latter with custom panels in a matching laminate, creating a vertical end piece. *Courtesy of David Taylor.*

An Artist in Manhattan

An artist's kitchen in Manhattan...what could be smaller? Benatar's objective was to utilize the available space to maximize the storage spaces and to create a design that integrates the kitchen with the living spaces of the apartment.

Victoria Benatar closed the existing side entrance and created a new center opening to the living/dining room with a wooden frame to match the new wooden cabinetry to the ceiling. All the appliances used are American brands in black to match the new absolute black floors and countertop. The black appliances, the cherry wood cabinetry, and the light blue walls result in an elegant kitchen. *Courtesy of David Taylor.*

Benatar added an undercabinet light and mirrored backsplash to create shadow and reflections that increased the light sources and the drama of the space. *Courtesy of David Taylor.*

Innovative Lighting Solution

The client's objective for their small 80 square foot city kitchen was to create a contemporary kitchen that permitted maximum storage space. They also asked for the floor tiles to continue beneath the cooktop. After careful space planning, the clients agreed that Tere Bresin should move the kitchen to allow for a dining room in front of the window where the original kitchen was. This move created a u-shaped kitchen.

Beret Design Group brought in a superior group of craftsmen to execute all aspects of the project, including demolition, lighting installation, completion of architectural moldings, and new walls as well as kitchen cabinets. The cabinet layout allowed for the use of a four burner cook top, a wall oven over a microwave, a Sub-Zero refrigerator, and upper cabinets that went to the ceiling to allow for maximum storage. The new kitchen included an under counter water purifier, sleek Italian hood over the stovetop, dishwasher, and double sink. A low voltage mono rail from the tech lighting system, using 50 watt MR16 lamps in satin nickel and field shaped into a gentle curve, provided overhead ambient lighting. Alklincs halogen lighting achieved under counter lighting.

The floor used 18" x 18", charcoal, Cotto D'Este marble on a diagonal. A combination of Giallo Serape and 3/4" mosaic gray glass tiles created the dramatic backsplash. The ultimate solution for this elegant kitchen revolved around the mix of an innovative yet practical lighting solution and a careful blending of hard surfaces.

Courtesy of Tere Bresin, ASID.

Chicago Loft Project

SieMatic and de Giulio Kitchen Design created the kitchen for this new Chicago loft. The client has one of the largest collections of Inro, a Japanese art form of the 16th and 17th century, in the world and displays this artwork throughout the home. The client wanted to maintain the feeling of open space.

The design intent for the kitchen was to be interesting yet undemanding, as it was visible to the rest of the home. The result allowed the furnishings and collections of the client to be more prominent than the kitchen itself.

De Giulio used a subtle palette of oak and stone (both granite and limestone) throughout to give a sense of warmth and texture. He designed a La Cornue range, along with a combination of cabinets set into plaster recesses in the cook top/range area. He constructed a simple plaster range hood over the cook area and eliminated the wall cabinets adjacent to the left and right of the range so as not to compete with any of the artwork collection. *Photography by Paul Schlismann.*

Open shelving at ceiling level integrates more art pieces into the kitchen. Custom automatic doors below the cabinets allow for a pass through into the walk-in pantry. Shelving, wine coolers, and a simple, unframed sanded glass entry door highlight the pantry. *Photography by Paul Schlismann.*

A long island, designed to permit seating, connects to a structural column clad in oak panels. The column includes book and artifact shelving to provide for additional display. To give a dramatic effect and Asian feel to the kitchen, de Guilio designed Mikado suspension lighting by Artemide above the island and in the space. *Photography by Paul Schlismann.*

Boston Penthouse

Clean, crisp lines characterize this kitchen designed by Dalia. The custom-tailored kitchen minimizes drudgery and maximizes the delight of the scene.

On entering the kitchen, the visitor is immediately drawn to the dramatic view of the city, which is framed by this contemporary kitchen. The world outside gives this kitchen, by Dalia, its color. *Courtesy of D. Peter Lund.*

The clean up center revolves around the very large, under-mounted sink. Its reduced height reduces the need to lift heavy pots up. It also can fit large objects such oven trays. *Courtesy of D. Peter Lund.*

A panel that matches the cupboards conceals the dishwasher. *Courtesy of D. Peter Lund.*

Appliances are built in. *Courtesy of D. Peter Lund.*

The cooking center is placed against the wall. Located away from the main traffic areas, it is surrounded by useful counters. *Courtesy of D. Peter Lund.*

The food prep center allows for coordinated action: rolling of dough, chopping, and general prepping. The drawers are organized to meet all requirements. *Courtesy of D. Peter Lund.*

You don't have to tumble through all those hand-me-downs and gadgets to find the right tool here. *Courtesy of D. Peter Lund.*

Cupboards are attractive. *Courtesy of D. Peter Lund.*

But they are also efficient workhorses. *Courtesy of D. Peter Lund.*

A small kitchen requires creative storage. *Courtesy of D. Peter Lund.*

Rounded corners make a cook's life easier – and less painful. *Courtesy of D. Peter Lund.*

The food storage center is less than a step away from the island. The refrigerator next to the tall pantry unit is reverse-hinged. The island becomes the landing area, where the homeowner can place and distribute the groceries. *Courtesy of D. Peter Lund.*

A small hanging television helps the cook maintain connection with the outside world. *Courtesy of D. Peter Lund.*

The lights can be lowered and raised. Their very discreteness allows the city to take center stage. *Courtesy of D. Peter Lund.*

A city that is seen from a penthouse cannot be hidden. *Courtesy of D. Peter Lund.*

The Asian Influence

Our culture can influence the style of kitchen.

Cupboards can be attractive and sources of illumination. *Courtesy of D. Peter Lund.*

Dalia's style in this Asian kitchen is simple – almost stark – but nonetheless beautiful. *Courtesy of D. Peter Lund.*

Efficient storage depends on having a
master plan. *Courtesy of D. Peter Lund.*

The peninsula can become the buffet. *Courtesy of D. Peter Lund.*

The Long, Thin Kitchen

Dalia worked with a narrow kitchen space in this unit.

A very basic layout should be kept as compact as possible. *Courtesy of D. Peter Lund.*

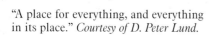

"A place for everything, and everything in its place." *Courtesy of D. Peter Lund.*

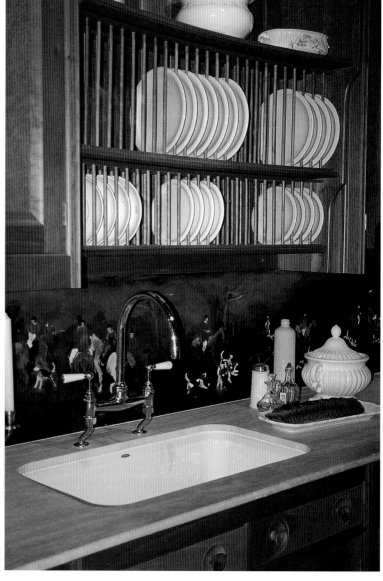

Opposite the preceding wall cabinet is this one using wicker baskets for sliding storage. *Courtesy of D. Peter Lund.*

The kitchen is small but attractive. *Courtesy of D. Peter Lund.*

The dining area is also small. *Courtesy of D. Peter Lund.*

Kitchen planning is simply a matter of common sense. *Courtesy of D. Peter Lund.*

The Farm Kitchen

The farmhouse style has moved to the city with Dalia.

This farm kitchen has a large wine rack, which takes up most of one wall. *Courtesy of D. Peter Lund.*

Natural colors, the earthy shades, look best in this style. *Courtesy of D. Peter Lund.*

The key to this style is simplicity. *Courtesy of D. Peter Lund.*

The farmhouse kitchen today can even include a hand pump. *Courtesy of D. Peter Lund.*

Boston Wharf Kitchen

A cook's kitchen is an efficient, hard-working room that must be planned and organized to the last detail. Plenty of workspace and a generous area surrounding the sink are essential. As Dalia says, "Good cooks automatically clean up as they go along." It is even more important to clean up when the kitchen is integrated with the living space in an elegant Boston waterfront condominium.

When you enter the residence, you are immediately aware of the light. *Courtesy of D. Peter Lund.*

Then you notice the view. *Courtesy of D. Peter Lund.*

What a view! *Courtesy of D. Peter Lund.*

The cooktop is surrounded by counter space. *Courtesy of D. Peter Lund.*

The visual impact of the urban kitchen depends largely on the color and texture of the fixtures and the fittings. A monochromatic color scheme unites the wall, floor, and cabinets. *Courtesy of D. Peter Lund.*

This kitchen is small and complete. *Courtesy of D. Peter Lund.*

The clean up area is across from the cooktop. *Courtesy of D. Peter Lund.*

Other than the flowers, the tiles are the only splash of color. *Courtesy of D. Peter Lund.*

The pantry and refrigerator stand side by side, waiting for that return trip from the supermarket. *Courtesy of D. Peter Lund.*

Small kitchens require tightly organized cupboards. *Courtesy of D. Peter Lund.*

Even the barstools are small. *Courtesy of D. Peter Lund.*

The overhead lighting is unobtrusive. *Courtesy of D. Peter Lund.*

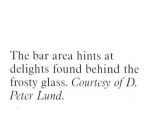

The bar area hints at delights found behind the frosty glass. *Courtesy of D. Peter Lund.*

Or good wines. *Courtesy of D. Peter Lund.*

Such as beautiful glasses. *Courtesy of D. Peter Lund.*

Contemporary Style

When the kitchen is small, you need to make every square inch work.

In this Dalia-designed kitchen, the ventilating system strikes its own decorative note. *Courtesy of D. Peter Lund.*

The food preparation area adjoining the stove is unusual. *Courtesy of D. Peter Lund.*

A well-designed kitchen organizes your kitchen storage for you. *Courtesy of D. Peter Lund.*

Adjustable shelving, sensible cupboards, and good counter space provide logical storage. *Courtesy of D. Peter Lund.*

Summer Condo

This summer retreat by Designs by Ria reflects the colors of summer.

This somewhat open space is comfortable for children and adults, who can share a small but functionally designed floor plan. *Courtesy of Zugcic Photographers.*

The lighted upper cabinets are used for glassware. The lighting enhances the lower area, which is suitable for seating with the addition of some barstools. The wall colors reflect the tones of the bamboo flooring, which was selected for ease of maintenance. *Courtesy of Zugcic Photographers.*

A close-up of the sink. *Courtesy of Zugcic Photographers.*

To complement the blue pearly granite countertop, 4" x 4" Ville Clear grey glass tile is used with a 1" x 1" Ville Blue sky glass tile for the kitchen backsplash. The sink is a stainless steel single bowl undermount Franke sink with a single lever Franke chrome faucet. The color of the crown molding is an accent used throughout the space. Pickled oak cabinetry and pewter hardware emphasize the casual feel. The trim on the bottom of the cabinets conceals the under-cabinet task lighting. *Courtesy of Zugcic Photographers.*

Contrast between Two San Francisco Kitchens

Two owners in the same 1900s San Francisco building retained Domus Design Group to design their kitchens. In these images, you see different designs for almost the same kitchens. After the firm designed the first kitchen, the owner of the unit beneath the one described in the first images approached Domus Group. This second client asked for the same layout but with a difference in finishes, details, and one other key component: she had no view but had lots of art.

Remodeled from a warren of small rooms, the first kitchen is layered with detail. Marble, moldings, trim, and lighting are utilized to produce a traditional kitchen with today's functionality. *Courtesy of Bruce Goff, ASID.*

Artfully crafted lighting fixtures – mixing brass, copper, and iron – highlight the end of the kitchen where a small breakfast area is arranged. The formal dining room is just a door away. *Courtesy of Bruce Goff, ASID.*

Using the same layout as the other kitchen in the building, Domus ensured that the owners would never mistake one for the other. Details in design, layout, and finishes assure individuality. *Courtesy of Bruce Goff, ASID.*

With no view but lots of art, the second client agreed with the decision to remove the large window that looked out on to the side of a building and received no light nor much ventilation. A clerestory window replaced it. Light marble, clean lined cabinets, and a natural color pallet allow a changing art collection to be moved throughout the house. A black-stained floor anchors the room. *Courtesy of Bruce Goff, ASID.*

The Cottage Cupboard

The existing kitchen had inadequate lighting, counter space, and storage space and was dark and dreary. Wanting an "Old World" look with maximum storage, the homeowners turned to Design Concepts Plus owner, Merrie Fredericks.

The stove area is the focal point from the entry hall. The hood was designed to enhance the Old World theme. A plate ledge around the top displays platters and plates. It also incorporates a granite shelf on the hood to store and display spices and condiments. A pair of pullout, angled fluted columns flank the stove to provide more storage.

The cabinetry includes four antique doors and large strap hinges. To give an additional display area, the cabinets do not reach the ceiling.

To create a softer look, beige tumbled marble and soft blue accent tiles complement the honed black granite. *Courtesy of Selective Photography.*

An open plate rack displays cups and dishware and functions as storage space. A single dishwasher drawer allows for additional pot storage below.

Originally, an old stained casement window was the only natural light source. The installation of a new casement window with glass shelving in front provides an additional display area and an element of privacy without blocking the light.

A more open feeling is given by the use of the French blue and gray tumbled stone tile on the kitchen and entry hall. *Courtesy of Selective Photography.*

To maximize the use of space, a recessed spice rack is built into the wall, separating the kitchen from the dining room. *Courtesy of Selective Photography.*

The homeowner wished to display an old Hoosier cabinet, an antique table, and a vintage mold collection. The antique wall cabinet in the entry area hangs above the antique table, where all the molds are displayed. Side wall-mounted lighting brightens the area. *Courtesy of Selective Photography.*

Penthouse Kitchen

Jonathan Isleib of Interdesign Limited renovated a Park Avenue penthouse kitchen.

A complete gutting of the kitchen was necessary, including the removal of a wall where the circular eating peninsula is pictured. A semi-custom cabinet system, Snaidero Co. of Italy, was selected for its brilliant metallic paint that helped open the spaces up and create a more expansive feel. European nickel stainless is used for countertops. Backsplashes are smoked mirror to subtly increase the expansiveness. The circular eating peninsula countertop is Marina Pearl granite. Floors are random width ash with a pickled finish. Lighting is by 12-volt, mini-recessed adjustable lights augmented by undercabinet lighting. *Courtesy of Woodruff & Brown Photography.*

Close-up view of sink and window to the north of Manhattan. An upper microwave oven is installed over the black glass cooktop. Dishwasher is beautifully integrated with the cabinets. The cabinet color is electrifying and so successful that the architect had his sailboat painted to match! *Courtesy of Woodruff & Brown Photography.*

Small Can Be Exciting

Playing off the client's contemporary art collection of bold lines and strong colors, Cherie Brown of Kitchens by Kleweno used a red metallic lacquer as the accent color to the tailored khaki and stainless steel. The black ripple doors, black toe, flyover, and granite add balance and texture to the palate.

The back splash is mirrored to reflect the opposite red wall and to add depth to the kitchen. The irregular island adds more counter space and a spot for a quick meal. *Courtesy of Greenspan Photography.*

The peninsula is raised to create some separation in the open floor plan. The black ripple cabinets provide a column at each end of the peninsula for both a visual as well as storage impact. *Courtesy of Greenspan Photography.*

Tribeca Triplex

The architect Mark Winkelman created this triplex apartment in Tribeca with project designer Rio Valledor of Downtown Group Architects. Keogh Design was hired to do the finishes and furniture throughout. In a true collaborative spirit, some finish suggestions resulted in design changes, while the existing building structure, along with architectural details, drove the final finish solutions. The client loved the mixture of cherry wood, steel, slate, and the colors yellow and rust.

In this photo, the block forms create a topography, both in the height and depth of the cabinetry, and intersecting planes. The extra deep cabinet with glass provides storage from both the dining and kitchen sides. The glass lightens up the massiveness of this particular cabinet, while providing the elegance needed for a more formal backdrop to the dining area. *Photo ©2003 Dan Muro.*

The client wanted little clutter showing in the kitchen. Two floating shelves on either side of the beautiful sculptured cooking hood fulfilled this wish. The kitchen design furthered the strong architectural statements of the rest of the triplex through forms playing against each other. *Photo ©2003 Dan Muro.*

On the kitchen side, the glass fronted dining cabinet provides an area for appliances used every day to be readily available, yet tucked away in their own niche. A frosted glass panel above the sink keeps the feeling of openness, yet hides the dirty dishes from the dining room. The pass through shelf is a helpful asset to any cook. *Photo ©2003 Dan Muro.*

More of the structural elements of this space are shown here. A floating steel stair to the upstairs living room is visible through the opening above the sink. *Photo ©2003 Dan Muro.*

The pantry off the kitchen stores most of the household's food and a dumbwaiter for delivering food up to the living room and downstairs to the teenagers' TV/game room. *Photo ©2003 Dan Muro.*

Upstairs, the living room fireplace area also receives the dumbwaiter. The architect believed the simple wheel and rope mechanism would remind us of the old building. The use of the original exposed beams and exposed bricks on the dining level, with a silver metallic painted wall against the steel stairs, combined with the skylight washing that wall is a wonderful play on old/new, rough/smooth, modernism and traditionalism. The lightness of the stair rail and the complex curve of the living room ceiling keep the spaces interacting with each other on all three levels. *Photo ©2003 Dan Muro.*

A pull out pantry is located next to the kitchen in the breakfast room and home office. It is great for housing breakfast food and late afternoon snacks. *Photo ©2003 Dan Muro.*

Trump Towers Modernism

This client wanted a clean, modern feel. The clean lines of this Trump Towers apartment, with no architectural enhancements, lent itself well to this concept. Upon entering the apartment, however, there was no sense of entry, and a guest could look directly into the kitchen. The client desired to have a larger kitchen for entertaining, but the building code restricted the kitchen size.

Keogh Design Inc. recommended the installation of a silk-paneled wall to make a more formal entry, while concealing the kitchen from direct view. A floating glass shelf with a mirror passing through defined the entryway further. A floating light reinforced the drama in this otherwise simple space.

To create an extended kitchen, Keogh Design created a working U-shaped counter with upper and lower cabinets, which functionally serves as storage as well as a "buffet" cabinet to the dining area.

The central room of this two-bedroom apartment was a simple box, with no clearly defined dining and living rooms. To visually translate the space into two areas, Keogh Design created a large triangular storage cabinet. This configuration draws visitors into the living space and defines the dining space as well.

The clients' collection of decorative objects is displayed on a built-in lighted cabinet with five sliding fabric panels, which allows the client to change the sections displayed by simply moving the fabric panels. *Photo ©2003 Dan Muro.*

Urban architecture has many restrictions, which can produce design opportunities. Common to urban architecture is slab construction, which means that you cannot chop into the slab to run new electrical wiring for ceiling lights. Here, the solution was to float wire lights, with a transformer connection back into the existing junction box, which cannot be moved.

The newly created entry wall houses a sculptural wall sconce. The new cabinetry in the extended kitchen has lights behind the glass doors, providing additional light to this area. *Photo ©2003 Dan Muro.*

Within the scale of the kitchen, small pin lights wash the face of the cabinetry, making it glow. Where possible, the cabinetry conceals appliances, such as the dishwasher. *Photo ©2003 Dan Muro.*

The use of elegant light maple wood and white stone with a mirrored backsplash helps to enhance this diminutive kitchen. The cabinet work was kept absolutely simple with no detail. This further increases the feeling of spaciousness. The mirrored backsplash also reflects the white counters, making the kitchen feel larger. *Photo ©2003 Dan Muro.*

East River Views

The clients were moving from a large suburban home with a typical kitchen into their dream Manhattan apartment. Their new kitchen had incredible views of the East River, but it had very little storage. The client wished to retain the feeling of openness between the kitchen and the den. Their desire to conceal the appliances, as well as to have their customary fully stocked pantry, added to the problems that needed to be solved by Keogh Design.

The den/breakfast area flows through to the kitchen by utilizing the pass through. Keogh Design installed an extra deep counter, which created additional storage on the dining side. The step down into the room means that when a guest is seated there, he/she is encased by a beautiful wall of wood and cannot see directly into the kitchen. *Photo ©2003 Dan Muro.*

The stereo/storage cabinet in the den repeats the wave glass used in the overheads. To maximize the feeling of spaciousness in the narrow den, Keogh Design created a thin wall cabinetry/display space. Angling the furniture also extended the depth of view, producing a dynamic interactive space. *Photo ©2003 Dan Muro.*

To integrate the den/family area with the kitchen, Keogh Design selected a light, natural maple for the kitchen and the den. The designer then combined natural cherry with the maple in the den wall unit for a more sophisticated look. *Photo ©2003 Dan Muro.*

The extra deep wall, which houses two pull out pantries, can be seen when passing from the den into the kitchen. This pantry solution actually houses almost as much food as the client had in her suburban house. *Photo ©2003 Dan Muro.*

The space on either side of the window is used to house appliances, which are easily available but out of sight.
Photo ©2003 Dan Muro.

Fully enclosed cabinets against the back wall give a wood backdrop to the view from the den.
Photo ©2003 Dan Muro.

The material solutions were kept to a minimum to maximize a feeling of spaciousness in this small kitchen. *Photo ©2003 Dan Muro.*

From Two to One

By combining two, small 1-bedroom apartments in this low ceiling building, the client could use two, small, back-to-back kitchens to create a real working kitchen that opened to the dining room. A primary objective was to use every single bit of space in this small area.

Once the normal appliances and sink were installed, not much counter space remained. Keogh Design opened up the wall to the dining space (formally the living room of the old apartment) and put in an additional buffet/counter. *Photo ©2003 Dan Muro.*

Typically, in urban apartments, columns and pipes appear that cannot be moved. The new design used the column in the kitchen as a bulletin board, which allowed the counter to wrap around. This arrangement provided further serving space on the dining side as well as an art wall. A slab ceiling drove Keogh Design to create soffits that concealed lighting around the kitchen and created a place to attach wire lighting for a new light to be positioned over the dining table. The new configuration removed the kitchen pipe from a wall and floated it, which allowed for an additional 2' of linear storage in the kitchen. *Photo ©2003 Dan Muro.*

At the front of the kitchen at the window, a niche over the heating unit allowed the creation of a small eating counter as well as a shallow appliance storage cabinet. To the left of the appliance counter, sliding translucent screens created a baby's room and allowed light into the dining room. Since the wall between the kitchen and dining room could be opened, fresh air was available through the kitchen window, and cross ventilation could be achieved by simply sliding the glass door open. *Photo ©2003 Dan Muro.*

A translucent "aged" glass keeps the feeling of openness to the kitchen. The normally unusable corner of the kitchen was utilized by opening the cabinet to the dining side, making the column appear as a useful form instead of an impediment. *Photo ©2003 Dan Muro.*

At the other end of the dining room, Keogh Design created a small office with wine storage. An open window (seen with a sheer fabric hanging on page 70) allows for a view and air circulation. *Photo ©2003 Dan Muro.*

A Design Opportunity

When this New York City family combined two apartments into one, they created this kitchen/family room/office. The office was the former master bedroom and bath. The miniscule kitchen had almost no counter space. The growing family required the addition of counter space and storage to the kitchen. They called in Keogh Design.

The wall behind the sink held plumbing pipes for all the apartments above this one. Keogh Design had another "design opportunity"! *Photo ©2003 Dan Muro.*

Taking advantage of this design obstacle, Keogh Design wrapped the kitchen around the wall of the plumbing. This move instantly created extra counter space within the kitchen area and an eating counter as well. The other side of the wrapped counter serves as a buffet space and walk through to the small dining area. A mirrored backsplash helps this interior wall to disappear – an inexpensive solution! *Photo ©2003 Dan Muro.*

The curved counter and new undermount sink doubled the amount of counter space in this newly constructed apartment building. Since the kitchen cabinetry was also new, the client desired to utilize that cabinetry as much as possible. Because Keogh Design was combining two existing apartments, they were able to salvage many of the cabinets, only building a few to fill in the gaps.

Using this cabinetry was like a big puzzle with some interesting results. Over the sink, a certain length of cabinetry was needed. This length existed with a short cabinet, which led to shallow shelving below, conveniently housing spices, oils, etc., while providing an open feeling over the sink. Again, the mirror backsplash provides a sensation of spaciousness over the sink. *Photo ©2003 Dan Muro.*

Another design problem that required solution was separating the kitchen from the dining room during a dinner party. Keogh Design added crown molding throughout the apartment for a traditional feel. Outside the kitchen, Keogh Design pulled this crown away from the wall to allow a "moving" art wall to close off the kitchen. *Photo ©2003 Dan Muro.*

The former master bedroom closet was the basis of the pantry closet. During demolition, Keogh found that there was sufficient space in this pipe area to carve out an area for book and wine storage. *Photo ©2003 Dan Muro.*

A Scandinavian Jewel

When Tuulikki Loring began work on this 10' x 11' kitchen, the owners ate in the dining room. She turned it into a sunlit, eat-in kitchen that also acted a showcase for the owner's collectibles.

Previously, the back hall to the living room was a pantry, and there wasn't any access to the living room. Tuulikki broke through the wall, giving access, and turned the pantry closet into a sunlit bar. *Courtesy of D. Peter Lund.*

Copper antiques decorate this alcove wall. *Courtesy of D. Peter Lund.*

The garden scene is always changing, ever-entertaining. *Courtesy of D. Peter Lund.*

Storage is key in this tiny kitchen. *Courtesy of D. Peter Lund.*

The kitchen appears to be larger because of the above-counter, white painted cabinets. *Courtesy of D. Peter Lund.*

The kitchen is the birthplace of many good things. *Courtesy of D. Peter Lund.*

The peninsula allows people to eat in the kitchen. It also houses the second oven. *Courtesy of D. Peter Lund.*

Some more collections. The wooden pieces are Finnish. *Courtesy of D. Peter Lund.*

The view from the dining room. Tuulikki widened the doorway to let in more light. *Courtesy of D. Peter Lund.*

This colorful kitchen basks in the winter sun. *Courtesy of D. Peter Lund.*

Nature rules. *Courtesy of D. Peter Lund.*

Built to Last

Nancy Mullan, ASID, CKD, faced a formidable task: to remodel and reconfigure a galley kitchen in a city apartment to reflect the personalities of "empty nesters," who loved cooking and entertaining family and friends. The kitchen opened into both the dining room and the foyer so it had to be stylish as well as functional. Its perimeter could not be expanded except at great expense.

Real limestone and tumbled marble are combined here with "solid-surface limestone" on the countertops. The kitchen was personalized with customized cabinetry and decorative painting, including a "carved" Latin inscription running around the top of the room that includes the owners, family members, the designer, and others. It concludes with Horace's phrase, "Eheu fugace anni" (alas, the fleeting years). *Courtesy of Bill Holt.*

Mullan's design features cabinets of varying depths, which makes the overall space feel larger yet provides maximum storage. *Courtesy of Bill Holt.*

The stainless steel undermount sink is well equipped with a routed drainboard cut into the counter top, pull-out trash container, and slide-out stepstool. The handle of the sponge drawer doubles as towel bar. The backsplash behind the sink is a series of 2" squares of tumbled marble set into a geometric pattern. *Courtesy of Bill Holt.*

A floor-to-ceiling glass-sided cabinet holds glassware and dishes in what would have been dead space. *Courtesy of Bill Holt.*

The 6' 6" Wide Kitchen

This small sun-filled kitchen is such an integral part of this one-bedroom terrace apartment that it had to be as elegant and sophisticated as the other rooms. Nancy Mullan selected color-washed canvas for the wallcovering. The pale limestone floor with green tumbled marble inserts is set diagonally to visually widen the narrow space. The cabinets and moldings are hand painted to blend with the limestone.

Nancy Mullan used visual tricks to make the space seem wider than its 6' 6". It has elegant neoclassic motifs and hand-carved mahogany counter tops and backsplashes as well as an 18" dishwasher and 24" integrated refrigerator. *Courtesy of Phillip Ennis, www.phillip-ennis.com.*

The raised panel frameless cabinets have a brushed paint finish and handpainted designs taken from the same Pompeian fresco source as the backsplash carving. Many cabinets, as well as their crown moldings, have been radiused to soften the look and increase the sense of space. *Courtesy of Phillip Ennis, www.phillip-ennis.com.*

The 18" dishwasher painted to match the cabinetry is large enough for a single person and most couples. The canvas wallcovering comes in widths up to 10' so most walls can be done without a seam. A slide-in stepstool provides instant access to upper shelves, important in a small kitchen. The refrigerator with freezer beneath is fully integrated into the wall. *Courtesy of Phillip Ennis, www.phillip-ennis.com.*

Countertops and backsplashes are mahogany with a marine finish that permit normal use. The hand-carved designs are inspired by the Pergolesi prints on the wall. *Courtesy of Phillip Ennis, www.phillip-ennis.com.*

The marine finish on the mahogany countertop makes it completely waterproof – notice the drainboard cut into it. The undermount sink boasts a pop-up drain so hands never need touch the water! The sponge drawer turns usually lost space into a handy hideaway for ugly but necessary cleaning accessories. *Courtesy of Phillip Ennis, www.phillip-ennis.com.*

A Curve on Tradition

   Historic homes are lovely, but space can be at a premium. The clients were Doreen Fair Westfall, of Eclipse Design Studio, Ltd., an interior designer, whose concern for aesthetics was equal to her concern for function, and her husband, a passionate cook, who had an uncompromising list of appliances (eight of them)! The goal presented to designer Jennifer Rand was to include all the appliances, have adequate storage, lots of counter space, and room for two cooks, and maintain an aesthetically pleasing view from the adjacent room!

This apartment is located near Louisburg Square, a charming neighborhood in the heart of Boston. Like many historic homes, every square inch of space is valued. *Courtesy of D. Peter Lund.*

The home was lovely. The kitchen was a U-shaped room, 9' x 9', with a curved wall pass through to the living/dining area. Low ceilings and exposed pipes and ducts made the space especially challenging. *Courtesy of D. Peter Lund.*

Details. *Courtesy of D. Peter Lund.*

The couple experimented with several layouts and selected the one that provided the most storage and work surfaces. A half-moon lazy Susan, utensil dividers, pullout spice/oil shelves, and a large tray cabinet extended for an access panel to plumbing maximized the base storage. *Courtesy of D. Peter Lund.*

The wall cabinets were built to completely conceal the existing ductwork behind their front frames. *Courtesy of D. Peter Lund.*

Panels or below eye level placement concealed the appliances. *Courtesy of D. Peter Lund.*

Every bit of space was used. *Courtesy of D. Peter Lund.*

Polished granite counters, stainless steel accents, and a glass mosaic backsplash tile add a cutting-edge to the traditional theme. *Courtesy of D. Peter Lund.*

Rich cherry cabinetry with recessed panel doors blended with the clients' dining furniture. *Courtesy of D. Peter Lund.*

San Francisco Fogs and the West-Facing Window

"Give me a light and airy space with professional quality appliances and separate work areas for two people," the new owner requested.

This 1929 kitchen in San Francisco's Pacific Heights retained its original dimensions and cabinetry until this major remodel. Measuring 11' wide x 13' long x 8' in height, it had been "remodeled" once before when the appliances were changed and ceramic tile applied to the floor and walls. With one west-facing window and San Francisco fogs, this kitchen was dark until afternoon.

With its small size, lack of natural light, and low ceiling, the new owners found the kitchen a depressing spot. The city building department nixed expansion. Creative use of existing space was the only solution. They turned to Virginia Smith of Sanders Smith Associates.

A butler's pantry adjoined the east kitchen wall, connecting the dining room and kitchen. The architect and Sanders Smith Interior Design decided to incorporate this area into the kitchen. With its east-facing window, more natural light was available. Then they discovered that a 9' 6" ceiling lurked above the existing 8' ceiling. They were ecstatic! *Courtesy of John Canham.*

With its 11' width, the kitchen was too narrow for an island, but a peninsula was possible. With the peninsula roughly separating the space shared by the kitchen and pantry, a second work area was born.

The south wall contains base cabinets with sinks and dishwashers with wall hung cabinets above. The opposing wall held all tall items, a 48" refrigerator, double ovens and warming drawer, pantry, and storage for casual dining.

In the new ceiling, speakers provide surround sound, and recessed fixtures furnish ambient lighting. Task lighting is under the wall cabinets.

Sanders Smith specified custom cabinetry that was built both deeper and taller than stock cabinets since the clients were tall and wanted to maximize counter space. The white painted wood cabinets appear similar to those originally in the kitchen. The expanded ceiling height allowed for generous use of crown moldings, an element missing in the original kitchen.

The base cabinet of the peninsula serves two functions. In addition to storage, it incorporates a radiator, the kitchen's only heat source. *Courtesy of John Canham.*

The cayenne-colored vein in the granite selected for the countertops and backsplashes was the inspiration for the striking wall color. The oak herringbone floor pattern matches the existing floors elsewhere in the home. Small oriental carpets define the two work areas and contribute a touch of softness to the room. A French fabric fashioned into Roman window shades complements the wall color.

The clients are thrilled with their new kitchen and somewhat astounded that their wish list was incorporated into this very defined area. *Courtesy of John Canham.*

Philadelphia Row-House

This historic, Center City Philadelphia home presented some unique challenges. The main thoroughfare to the second floor and to the exterior courtyard is directly through the kitchen, narrowing the 20' space to just 6 1/2' wide.

Abby Schwartz Associates developed a simple "L" shaped plan that incorporated the owner's love of clean lines, natural materials, and contrasting color into an elegant, functional, and modern space. The integration of flush maple cabinets, honed granite countertops, black stained wood flooring, stainless steel surfaces, abstract art, and muslin Roman shades resulted in a serene simplicity.

A view towards the kitchen.
Courtesy of Rob Ikeler.

A view from the stairs to the food preparation and clean up area. *Courtesy of Rob Ikeler.*

This is a long narrow kitchen. *Courtesy of Rob Ikeler.*

The view from the dining room. *Courtesy of Rob Ikeler.*

View of the dining room. *Courtesy of Rob Ikeler.*

The new stove and custom stainless backsplash and hood.
Courtesy of Rob Ikeler.

Keyhole Kitchen

The existing kitchen was a 7' x 11' room with two doors impinging on the workspace, one leading from the central hall and the other leading into the formal dining room. Dating from the 1960s, it was L-shaped with a stranded, overly large refrigerator.

The client asked for a colorful kitchen with elements of both traditional and contemporary design. She wanted floral motifs, soft contours, and brilliant colors.

The dramatic shape of the new kitchen designed by Sutton Design reflects a more organic, less machined sensibility, which used curved cabinet fronts at several locations. At other locations, the cabinetry is curved to soften entry to and exit from the space.

Patrick Sutton's new plan removed the non-structural wall separating the kitchen from the dining room and extending it well into the former dining area. An exterior window became a door, which leads to a new screened-in porch constructed of tropical hardwoods. Other windows were shortened to allow cabinetry placement.

The kitchen workspaces are divided into use zones, with each item of cabinetry within each zone customized to fulfill assigned functions. Most cabinets suggest their function by their location or detailing. The client is 5' tall, so many counters are below "standard" height.

Sutton used different materials to fulfill specific functions. Since teak performs well as a draining surface that won't damage delicate china and crystal, it is used for the wet counter and the draining rack. Stone is used where heat and abuse are of concern: the low appliance center, the cooktop area, and the long work surface island. Durable end-grain butcher block is strictly for chopping, and decorative hardwoods, like maple and walnut, are used for light-duty counters.

This image shows off the dramatic keyhole shape and the impressive stainless steel pot rack. Note the unusual custom-turned legs of the island. *Courtesy of suttondesign interiors llc.*

The main storage areas of the kitchen, as well as the bar area, feature maple and cherry cabinetry. The audio/video system is the central system for the entire house. The television pulls out and swivels for viewing from anywhere in the kitchen. *Courtesy of suttondesign interiors llc.*

The sink area has a dramatic curvature. *Courtesy of suttondesign interiors llc.*

The main work areas of the kitchen – wet zone, chopping station, and cooking – have some fun design touches. In the island and dishwasher area are hand-painted floral motifs. The light fixture shade comes through the center of the pot rack (not visible in this photo); the shade features the same leaf patterning in green and yellow as the island. The teak draining rack drains onto canted stone, in turn draining onto teak, in turn draining into the stainless steel sink. *Courtesy of suttondesign interiors llc.*

The butcher block top of the chopping station has a waste chute for cuttings. A custom-turned maple cap is fitted to the top of the chute, while a removable stainless-steel pan in the drawer catches the cuttings. The custom kitchen table is in the background, as well as the door leading out to the new covered porch. The striped drapes were made from vintage Scalamandre silk owned by the client. *Courtesy of suttondesign interiors llc.*

The high-quality cabinetry work, particularly the curved profile executed both on the cabinet and on the custom handles, is clearly visible. Note that even small touches like the backsplash pieces in this kitchen are detailed for interest. *Courtesy of suttondesign interiors llc.*

The floral motif is worked into the kitchen in various ways. The cabinet glass has a custom etched floral pattern; the Roman shades are custom made from sourced fabric; the client's china features floral elements. The wall and cabinet colors are organic yellows. *Courtesy of suttondesign interiors llc.*

The radiused plate dowel rack, constructed of teak, accommodates plates and dishes of different sizes. Wet items are intended to drip on to the stone and teak surfaces below, which are, in turn, sloped towards the undermount stainless steel sink. *Courtesy of suttondesign interiors llc.*

Lake Front Residence

Designed by Thielsen Architects, Inc., P.S. and built by Willkens Construction, this lake front residence emphasizes clean lines and contemporary regional forms. These two elements are clearly visible in the kitchen on the home's main level.

Viewed from the living room through the series of beams and columns, the kitchen blends seamlessly with the rest of the home. The maple paneled dining room at the right echoes the maple cabinets of the kitchen. The granite-topped buffet is illuminated by three pendant lights, as is the granite-topped island. *Courtesy of Krogstad Photography.*

The kitchen is a study in clean lines and efficiency. The space is washed in natural light from a large skywall and west facing windows that create a balanced light, perfect for cooking and entertaining. *Courtesy of Krogstad Photography.*

From the dining room, the spatial flow to the kitchen is clear and unencumbered, yet it is set apart by the island and the columns. In the evening, under-cabinet lights enliven the corrugated metal backsplash. *Courtesy of Krogstad Photography.*

Set on the eastern shore of Seattle's Lake Washington, the lake front residence is an urban beach house that makes use of contemporary forms and materials. The corrugated metal of the backsplash in the kitchen is drawn from the corrugated metal of the exterior. *Courtesy of Krogstad Photography.*

Frame and Release Kitchen

The objective in this kitchen was to maximize storage and countertop space while maintaining visual openness. The lower cabinets are framed by continuous countertops or "planes," while the upper cabinets are manipulated frames that create spaces for traditional cabinetry and fixed shelving. Architect Rupinder Singh of Mimar Design calls this a Frame and Release kitchen.

The upper cabinets are compositionally arranged within frames that unfold to create shelving. *Courtesy of Rupinder Singh.*

The bottom cabinets are neatly tucked in beneath a wider than normal countertop, seemingly extending the space of the kitchen in perspective. *Courtesy of Rupinder Singh.*

A view of cabinets at the range.
Courtesy of Rupinder Singh.

Frames of space unfold and invite the viewer into the kitchen. A hint of framed cabinets on the left alludes to a second set of cabinetry. *Courtesy of Rupinder Singh.*

The small kitchen offers a compact yet efficient distribution of kitchen functions (cooking, cleaning, and reheating). *Courtesy of Rupinder Singh.*

Café Penne

This kitchen, created by Penny Chin of Elements in Design, makes you reminisce about charming places you have been or want to be in!

This narrow island features the wine refrigerator and several base cabinets with accessibility from both sides. *Courtesy of Jim Preston.*

To add interest, the designer included a 45" high counter top, which houses a built-in space saver microwave at just the right height – a height that is safer than microwaves installed over the cook tops. *Courtesy of Jim Preston.*

Another must-have appliance – a warming drawer tucked under the dishwasher. The kitchen has working and serving counter space. *Courtesy of Jim Preston.*

The theme for the kitchen began with the painting of this café scene. *Courtesy of Jim Preston.*

Chin elected to increase the visual effect of this small kitchen with a mural painted on the garage door. A red telephone booth painted on the laundry room door conceals a stacking washer and dryer. *Courtesy of Jim Preston.*

Fine Grain

The challenge here was renovating a historical home to suit the taste of a contemporary owner. The new design exposed the kitchen to the living areas, calling for a design that would not only complement but enrich the rest of the spaces in the home. Using carefully chosen cabinetry, the Kitchen Design Studio (KDS) transformed this kitchen from a cold, uninviting space to a warm, welcoming space without compromising its elegant, contemporary lines. Using warm natural cherry cabinetry, rich granite tops, and reflective stainless steel appliances, KDS transformed the kitchen into a functional and attractive design.

The custom kitchen cabinetry, created by the craftsman of K.D. and Steele Cabinetry is the quality of fine furniture, yet functional. *Courtesy of Kimball Derrick, CKD of the Kitchen Design Studio.*

The drawers under the glass cupboard and the upward-lifting cupboards or "garages" to their right are attractive storage vehicles. *Courtesy of Kimball Derrick, CKD of the Kitchen Design Studio.*

The appliances are integrated into the design. Note the warming racks on the stove and the second sink in the island. *Courtesy of Kimball Derrick, CKD of the Kitchen Design Studio.*

This kitchen reflects the contemporary style of the home, but honors the historical nature as well. *Courtesy of Kimball Derrick, CKD of the Kitchen Design Studio.*

Vacation Condominium Kitchen

Sydnie Barcenas of LVSB Designs planned this Las Vegas vacation condominium kitchen around the client's professional lifestyle. The couple can take the time to relax in between or on their way to their business commitments or their other home, while still being able to enjoy the entertainment that this city has to offer.

Double lazy Susan's beside the stove appear small, but they store small appliances in previously useless corner spaces. The convection range allows benefits of faster cooking for their busy lifestyle, while the Advantium microwave doubles as an extra oven. *Courtesy of James Lindstrom.*

A cabinet-depth refrigerator is enclosed to look like a built in, while the 18" wide wine cooler stores their collection until they return to the city to enjoy them. Undercounter and hanging halogen lights exude elegance. *Courtesy of James Lindstrom.*

The contemporary Shaker style, light maple, frameless cabinets allow maximum storage in limited space, harmonizing with the existing furniture. The pass-through bar is a great way to visit with the chef, share snacks, or enjoy a nice meal. *Courtesy of James Lindstrom.*

Kitchen/Party Prep Area

Patricia Davis Brown Fine Cabinetry integrated this small kitchen into an open plan design. The resulting safe, functional, personalized space incorporates imaginative design statements and aesthetically pleasing solutions.

Whether you need a second work station, a space from which to serve an informal buffet, or just a place to toss the day's mail, kitchen bars and islands are popular solution to the lack of kitchen space. *Courtesy of Patricia Davis Brown Fine Cabintry, Inc.*

A butler's pantry or party prep area is slightly off to the side. It is fully loaded with a bar sink, appliances, storage, and fancy surfaces. *Courtesy of Patricia Davis Brown Fine Cabintry, Inc.*

With the party prep area outside the kitchen's main work triangle, one family member can cook while another prepares drinks without getting in each other's way. *Courtesy of Patricia Davis Brown Fine Cabintry, Inc.*

Starting Anew

Nothing is more exhilarating in life than starting anew. This city kitchen is all about change: life in the city instead of the suburbs, living in a high-rise condo instead of a house, an open concept plan with views of both the lake and city lights instead of a traditional kitchen. Additionally, the couple plans to pursue an interest in fine wine and gourmet cooking.

They contracted with Laura Trujillo of Dybdahl's Classic Kitchens and Cabinetry to design their kitchen.

The open concept plan demanded a kitchen that looks as good as it functions. The creative use of color, shape, and detail makes this compact kitchen a focal point in the space. The gloss metallic blue paint finish of the base cabinetry reflects the lake view while the light wood glass finish of the upper cabinetry lightens and enlarges the area. Glass doors, stainless steel, and angled cabinets add sleek contemporary accents. *Courtesy of Joe DeMaio.*

Opposite Page:
Top: Pot and pan drawers under the cook top and the use of refrigerator and freezer drawers provide easy access. The Sub-Zero wine cooler stores their collection, guaranteeing the perfect serving temperature. The microwave is discreetly hidden behind a flip-up door. *Courtesy of Joe DeMaio.*

Bottom left: The contemporary styled cabinetry is loaded with convenience features. The corner base cabinet has "Magic Hardware" engineered to fully utilize what normally would be considered "dead space." When the cabinet door is opened, a mini swing-out pantry unit magically appears with interior lighting that makes all items easy to find. *Courtesy of Joe DeMaio.*

Bottom right: Glass doors, stainless steel, and angled cabinets add sleek contemporary accents. *Courtesy of Joe DeMaio.*

Feng Shui Kitchen

Jill Dybdahl, owner of Dybdahl's Classic Kitchens and Cabinetry, worked with Jackie Patricia, Feng Shui Master, on her kitchen. The goal was to create a kitchen in an existing small space, which would not only be beautiful and function well, but would also give Jackie a sense of serenity through its sensitivity to space.

Proper appliance selection played a major role in achieving not only a workable space but also an eye-pleasing end. Jill specified the Sub-Zero fully integrated 700 series because of its narrow width and because it has no mechanical parts visible. As a result, the 700TC melts into the design, leaving the space peaceable and beautiful.

Total integration of appliances was high priority to Jackie. In the resulting design, two strong horizontal lines dominate the room. The top of the 700TC's freezer drawers line up with the top of the standard base cabinets. This permits a continuous line of soft, pewter-colored base cabinets, which is important for the chi of the space. The upper doors were finished in birch with the grain wrapping horizontally, uninterrupted around the upper door of the 700TC, creating the second horizontal line in the room.

The adjacent Bosch dishwasher was fitted with two false drawer heads so that the horizontal theme would continue to flow without interruption from one appliance to the next.

Below: Jackie had visions of the kitchen being defined by strong horizontal lines. Soft gray painted base cabinets and natural birch wood veneer on the upper cabinets created horizontal flow.

Jill suggested running the birch wood grain horizontally around the room to accentuate the theme. The adjacent doors were built from the same wood flitch. The overall result was that of the unwrapping of a tree around the room hugging the fortunate cook with warmth. *Courtesy of Joe DeMaio.*

The countertops reinforced the horizontal theme. Jackie boldly put Corian lilac around a special order Stone Forest sink! The periwinkle color of the top continues up the backsplash, meeting the wall cabinets. The Corian counter gently joins the smooth honed-finished stone basin sink, creating a union that draws one to the area – now everyone wants to do the dishes!

Since the space is small and the owner does cook, storage was necessary. The counter to the right of the cooktop projects in front of the stationary portion of the sliding glass door to give more storage and seated counter area. By breaking the rules and placing cabinetry and the angled snack counter in front of the fixed side of the sliding glass door, Jill added more counter space. *Courtesy of Joe DeMaio.*

Jackie can lift the drop-down counter to the left of the sink for added counter space during cleanup. After the work is done, it can be dropped down again for added kitchen space, making a larger walkway to the dining room. *Courtesy of Joe DeMaio.*

On the opposite side of the room, Avonite Moon Dust was selected to blend with the gray hue of the base cabinets and stainless steel cooktop. The monochromatic run of cabinets and tops creates a peaceful surrounding for Jackie to prepare her meals.

The 27" wide Dacor double convection ovens were chosen for their outstanding performance and sleek appearance. Rounding the corner from the ovens is the Dacor gas cooktop with downdraft. Jackie considered the hood to be too obtrusive and wished to display artwork above the cooking surface. *Courtesy of Joe DeMaio.*

Small Yellow Kitchen

This kitchen is small, but Cheryl Casey Ross of Cross Interiors added all the amenities of a large kitchen: wine cooler, built-in refrigerator/freezer, dishwasher, built-in oven, warming drawer, and microwave (behind closed doors above the oven), a free standing professional range, and even a pot filler faucet by the range.

The tiles are hand-painted. Some were added on the inside of the glass fronted wall cabinets. There is under and over cabinet lighting. The century-old flooring was brought from France. It even has labels from areas where it was taken. *Courtesy of Leonard Lammi.*

The room had 3' added to make an eating area with seating in the bay window. *Courtesy of Leonard Lammi*

The island with its yellow limestone countertop was built as a piece of furniture, with a library shelf under it for cookbooks and an area to display baskets of fruit and vegetables. Electricity is available to the island on both sides. *Courtesy of Leonard Lammi.*

Gutting the Kitchen

This kitchen was too small, and the space was not well planned. Counters were too low to accommodate a dishwasher, and the space sized for the refrigerator allowed only a small unit. No counters were near the range, and a pantry was definitely needed. The kitchen door opened to a laundry room, which had only the standard washer/dryer/hot water heater arrangement. There were two overhead ceiling fixtures: one in the laundry, one in the kitchen. There were two small corner windows. The sink was on a clipped corner, with plumbing exposed behind a fabric skirt.

Cheryl Casey Ross of Cross Interiors solved these problems by gutting the whole area and starting over!

A broom closet, pantry, and counter spaces were added to the laundry room. The stacked washer and dryer and built-in clothes hamper make this room more functional. *Courtesy of Leonard Lammi.*

The clipped corner was squared off. The doorway was moved and arched to match an existing door. The pantry/laundry room is through the small arched doorway, which was copied from the original arched doorway. *Courtesy of Leonard Lammi.*

A new arched custom-made window over the sink adds much more light than the room previously had and opens wide to let in fresh air.

Recessed can lighting now distributes light evenly throughout the areas. Bright white custom cabinetry with a lacquer finish lightens and extends the space. The hand-painted imported French tiles are a counterpoint to the cabinets. *Courtesy of Leonard Lammi.*

Nantucket Style Kitchen

It was a small kitchen and dining area, with a sitting area directly outside the kitchen door in an atrium. Cheryl Casey Ross of Cross Interiors transformed it into a small jewelbox with a fountain.

The decorator lacquered the existing cabinets white, tiled the floors, and added beadboard. *Courtesy of Leonard Lammi.*

To enhance the cottage look, she added a chandelier to the dining room and decorated the walls with pictures and plates. *Courtesy of Leonard Lammi.*

After removing the cement slab from the outdoor dining area, she designed a garden area with stepping stones and ground cover. She added a fountain for charm and the soothing sound of running water. The view you see is from the kitchen door, one step from the kitchen. *Courtesy of Leonard Lammi.*

Personally Designed

The Basement Condo

This kitchen lies beneath the city streets.

The townhouse is one of those lovely old brick homes in a tree-shaded residential neighborhood. *Courtesy of D. Peter Lund.*

The miniscule kitchen fits under the stairs. *Courtesy of D. Peter Lund.*

Nicely equipped, it is filled with wedding presents. *Courtesy of D. Peter Lund.*

Storage is limited. There is a closet that no one is allowed to see that holds everything else. *Courtesy of D. Peter Lund.*

The flowers bloom on. *Courtesy of D. Peter Lund.*

The coffee is great. *Courtesy of D. Peter Lund.*

When there are only several guests, they can sit at the bar. *Courtesy of D. Peter Lund.*

When there are more, they can sit around this family heirloom. *Courtesy of D. Peter Lund.*

And watch the cabinet lights change color, outlining and electrifying the space.
Courtesy of D. Peter Lund.

When the weather turns warm, they can take their coffee outside to the sunken patio.
Courtesy of D. Peter Lund.

And sit, letting the world go by. *Courtesy of D. Peter Lund.*

The Development Kitchen

Throughout the United States, there are many standard edition kitchens.

Housing developments can be large, and sometimes you no longer feel like an individual. *Courtesy of D. Peter Lund.*

As in many kitchens, this window over the sink looks right at the neighbor. *Courtesy of D. Peter Lund.*

Counter space surrounds the stove. *Courtesy of D. Peter Lund.*

As you wash the dishes, you can look at your neighbor or your kids. Or perhaps you dream. *Courtesy of D. Peter Lund.*

The refrigerator is opposite the sink. *Courtesy of D. Peter Lund.*

The kitchen ends in a peninsula overlooking the family room. *Courtesy of D. Peter Lund.*

County Mouse

This small kitchen, ripe with color, has little modern technology.

Some styles are quite open. *Courtesy of D. Peter Lund.*

The table serves as the food prep area. *Courtesy of D. Peter Lund.*

The appliances are old. *Courtesy of D. Peter Lund.*

Farm market produce waits in a bowl. *Courtesy of D. Peter Lund.*

Such as this beautiful bowl of oranges. *Courtesy of D. Peter Lund.*

Colorful grace notes await us in this rural
atmosphere. *Courtesy of D. Peter Lund.*

Small Kitchen with Baby

This kitchen reflects the owners' warmth and charm.

Acres and acres of housing developments dot the landscape in the United States. *Courtesy of D. Peter Lund.*

The soft blue rug alleviates the plain lines. *Courtesy of D. Peter Lund.*

Interesting wall pieces, such as this old checkerboard, add sparks of interest. *Courtesy of D. Peter Lund.*

An antique pot holds well-used cooking utensils. The canisters are English Stilton cheese containers. *Courtesy of D. Peter Lund.*

The baby gets the corner. *Courtesy of D. Peter Lund.*

The double sink faces the side-by-side refrigerator. Both are necessary in a house with three children. *Courtesy of D. Peter Lund.*

Kitchen with Fireplace

A fireplace suggests an open hearth, rocking chairs, and marshmallows.

The kitchen lies behind the living room. *Courtesy of D. Peter Lund.*

You travel down a narrow byway. *Courtesy of D. Peter Lund.*

A scrubbed pine table sitting in the middle of the room is a nostalgic image. It is in keeping with the intimacy of the house. *Courtesy of D. Peter Lund.*

When storage is short, pots and pans can hang from the ceiling. *Courtesy of D. Peter Lund.*

An interesting plate breaks the monotony of the bricks. *Courtesy of D. Peter Lund.*

This blue door, which illuminates the room through its window-panes, exits to the patio. *Courtesy of D. Peter Lund.*

The chimney towers high, and not a creature is stirring. *Courtesy of D. Peter Lund.*

The sink and stove are surrounded by counter space. *Courtesy of D. Peter Lund.*

The Plumber's Kitchen

The owner, a skilled plumber, knew his kitchen could work better. His wife,
a gifted cook, agreed. She wanted granite countertops. He wanted a gas cooktop.
They kept the colors simple and light to make the room appear larger.

They retained the original room. They installed a Grohe faucet and a large sink that holds the biggest cookie sheets. *Courtesy of Siobhan Theriault.*

They installed a range that has a gas cook-top and electric oven and a large new vent, which exhausts to the outside. Their small house will no longer have odd kitchen aromas. The backsplash on the range is the same granite as the countertops. *Courtesy of Siobhan Theriault.*

They added glass to the top cabinet so to bring light and interest into the room. *Courtesy of Siobhan Theriault.*

They installed a Grohe faucet and a large sink that holds the biggest cookie sheets. *Courtesy of Siobhan Theriault.*

The cabinets trace the room's contour, making the room more interesting than the usual flat line of cabinets. *Courtesy of Siobhan Theriault.*

A Kitchen Renovation

My first kitchen had a bright yellow, early 1970s Formica counter. When we decided to tune into the 1990s, we installed tile. What a mistake for an inveterate cook, once-a-week baker, and haphazard cleaner!

At one point, we had even considered moving rather than redoing it again, but the neighborhood suited our needs; the property values were increasing; we like being here.

Of course, remodeling means no sink, no stove, workmen early in the morning, and dust, dust, dust!

Design

To help us rethink a kitchen that had been created from two, ancient, small rooms in a home in a historic district, we called in a full service kitchen remodeling company early in August. The company came with a kitchen designer: Jennifer Rand, whose work is seen in earlier in this book.

Kitchen design is a subjective process. What may be perfect for one family is far from perfect for another. In the two earlier renovations (1972 and 1991), we had relied on our judgment and that of the contractor. We had made many measurements, even scale drawings, but the cupboards were dark, the lighting poor, and the room was always cold.

Our kitchen is the busy active center of our lives. This time, we wanted the experts.

We got one. Jennifer gave us a long questionnaire developed by the National Kitchen & Bath Associates (NKBA): who was the cook, which hand did he/she use, what were the traffic patterns, did we have guests often? We found we learned a great deal about our habits and hopes, likes and dislikes. Appendix A contains much of this questionnaire.

She did preliminary measuring, concurred with our desire to enhance our view of the garden, and drew plans. We planned to eliminate the bar sink and move the sink from the side wall to the corner. That way, we could get the plumbing out of the ceiling and maybe gain some inches overhead.

Jennifer focused on our desire to keep the kitchen as a gathering place for a wide and varied number of activities. She added focal points and better lighting; she introduced us to new cupboards and counter material. So many decisions.

Luckily, Jennifer helped us decide. By the end of August, we were reviewing the proposal that delineated the work from demolition to materials.

We checked the contractor's references: how clean would they leave the job site, how long would we be without a kitchen (seven weeks!), would the former clients recommend the firm to their mother? (A resounding yes from all!)

By September, we had picked our middle-of-the-line cabinets, ceramic floor and backsplash, and granite counters. We planned to begin in mid-October. Then I broke my leg. Coincidentally, we learned that the kitchen probably couldn't be done in time for Christmas. We postponed the job until January.

By December, we had paid 80% of the final bill, but no work had begun. Against the advice of our friends (who were thinking of my prowess on the cane), we decided to move our kitchen to temporary quarters in the basement, where we had double wash tubs and counter space rather than into the dining room.

Tear Down Diary

January 2: Our houseguests leave; we empty the kitchen. We return from a trip to the airport and find that the water is turned off. Too bad, the dishwasher was half full. The gas went the next day.

We organize the basement to become our kitchen. We have a hot plate, microwave, electric fry pan, and coffeepot. If more than two items are plugged in, we blow fuses. The hot plate, which was my Dad's, is wonderful. The new appliances are delivered in a snowstorm and housed in the garage.

January 4: The cupboards are bare. We are now cooking in the basement, but the refrigerator is in the dining room. There's too much snow to get it through the back door to the basement.

January 5: The walls are tumbling down. The old appliances are removed. I had tried to find homes for them, but in all cases, other than the stove, no one wants my perfectly good, seven year old appliances or the solid, though faded, cabinets. It hurts to discard good equipment.

The kitchen is blocked off. To get lunch, Peter has to walk out the front door and go around the back to the basement to bring lunch back around. Not so bad if it was a nice spring day, but the snow is about a foot deep.

January 6: Vast excitement. The workmen find a door and window hidden under the plaster. The insulation we had blown in over the years never got into the cavities. No wonder we had problems with the cold. They also find a 4' wide firewall covering the chimney.

Under the ancient plaster, we find the reason that our kitchen had always been cold. *Courtesy of D. Peter Lund.*

The house is one large plaster dust ball. Everything is gray, even my plants on the third floor. It's embarrassing when the physical therapist brushes me off before beginning work on my leg.

The workmen find a 1923 *Boston Globe* hidden in the walls. The bathroom has four ceilings. I wonder about the previous homeowners. What were they like? What were their concerns? I begin work on our own time capsule.

January 7: The first day without workmen. Also the first day we can walk through the house again, wiping off dust as we go. Even the simple task of making a cup of coffee becomes a major undertaking without a kitchen.

January 9: Yesterday, we discussed the need for reframing the wall where the door and the window were found and the wall where the firewall was. Here, I thought the major decisions revolved around color of tiles!

Instead of reading the detailed contract at the showroom, we should have brought it and the final plans home and reviewed both while walking through the kitchen. The back hallway wall must be removed, and we need another central light switch and a switch for the outside lights. We should have specified these. The additional cost is $2200. The kitchen now costs about what we paid for the house in 1972. Oh my!

When the contractor said that they would move things out of the kitchen, I had assumed that meant moving them to where I wanted them – such as the refrigerator to the basement. Not true. Much to my annoyance, the refrigerator remains in the dining room. With all the snow and ice and our narrow doorways, the contractor doesn't want to attempt that move.

We learn from our mistakes. Everything should have been specified.

January 10: The electricians are here to rip out the old wires.

This photo shows the back hallway. The wall to the left will be removed. Note the wiring dripping down from the ceiling. *Courtesy of D. Peter Lund.*

We wanted the view from this window for our new kitchen. *Courtesy of D. Peter Lund.*

Installation

January 11: Saws scream. The studs are going up.

January 16: The electricians install the lights. Many of them. How nice as my eyesight deteriorates. I never realized that undercounter lighting would make such a difference. The carpenter returns.

January 22: The plumbing work begins. The changed position of the sink means that we can raise the ceiling four inches. We are delighted. No longer will my taller friends be forced to stoop.

The D-shaped sink fits nicely into the corner. Counters surround it. *Courtesy of D. Peter Lund.*

January 26: The security alarm guy came. Luckily, everything is still open. Too bad we didn't realize he should be called. It would have been easier if he were here with the carpenter.

January 29: The electrical and the plumbing work has been done for almost a week. We've been waiting for the building inspector. Today, he came for three minutes, saying we need to add firestops. He didn't seem to be concerned about the single 4" x 4" beam supporting the second floor. We can skip a vertical support.

The insulation is in. Such a difference already in the warmth of the room.

February 1: We go away and return to dark gray wallboard. The kitchen looks small again. They forgot to put in the time capsule with the 1923 *Boston Globe.* Our friends joke that they fed us all fall while I lay in bed, and they are feeding us all winter as the project continues. We are so lucky to have them.

February 4: It is Sunday, but the plasterers are here at 8AM.

February 5: The kitchen is plastered the day of the "Northeaster." The house feels cold, wet, and damp. The kitchen looks a lot bigger now that it is white. Ideally, Peter should prime the walls before the cupboards are installed.

February 6: Thanks to the storm, the week is quiet. We cook Monday night, which means blowing fuses. Both Samson and I can get down the stairs now.

February 9: We go away for 24 hours, hoping that the subfloor would be installed while we were gone. No such luck. The carpenters arrive after we are home, and the snowstorm has begun. Peter cooks scallops almandine for dinner. We are getting pretty good on that hot plate.

Dust clings to everything, even the leaves of the smallest plants. The garage is filled with appliances and materials. Sometimes it is hard to be polite, especially when I can't park in the driveway and have to limp down the street, avoiding the ice.

February 12: The cabinets are being installed. Their light color tends to brighten and visually enlarge the space. On the other hand, they are so sturdy that they take up more room than I thought they would. The utility cabinet certainly will not hold the vacuum.

February 14: Peter is priming the walls; I am selecting laundry room wallpaper. We can see the end. You certainly do need your friends unless you love take-out.

February 16: Decisions, decisions. Should the woodwork match the paint or the cupboards? Amazing how the space for the microwave just works. Tonight, I labor downstairs over my two burner hot plate making barley pilaf with shitake and oyster mushroom sauce.

February 20: The new corner pantry and back hall look great.

We now get the light from the north window and have a big new counter area. *Courtesy of D. Peter Lund.*

Our Sub-Zero refrigerator drawers are underneath the new counter. They make a nice addition to our refrigerator. *Courtesy of D. Peter Lund.*

The stove and microwave have taken the place of the former sink. *Courtesy of D. Peter Lund.*

I gave the contractor a closing date. He said the floor man was coming. The washing machine is now out of action. Great. Now the laundry gets taken to the neighbor. It snows and snows. Did I say how I hate the refrigerator in the dining room?

February 21: We have two for dinner tonight and two more for wine beforehand. I figured how to cook my potatoes beforehand and just warm them in the toaster oven. I had made the sauce for the beef that morning. Peter grills the beef; I sauté zucchini and make a decent bananas foster. Only blew the fuses twice. A lot of dishes to troop up the stairs, but we manage.

February 23: They are laying the floor. We can't walk on it. Dogs are going nuts. The back door doesn't close for some weird reason.

March 5: We seem to have been on hold, until I told the contractor that we were having a party. The scramble began. We went away, and the refrigerator got moved from the dining room to the garage and the new one installed. They even loaded the food from one into the other. The icemaker is missing. Great. It begins to snow…again!

March 7: Eighteen inches later. In comes the granite countertop. It's beautiful. The plumber points out that the dishwasher can't fit under the counter. The kitchen contractor says he is wrong, but he is right. The tile man shouldn't have tiled under it. We have the dinner party; everyone washes dishes.

The microwave doesn't work. GE says we need a technician. Peter is greatly annoyed.

I begin refilling the cabinets and find that now we have three of everything: three bags of apricots, three bags of rice cakes, three bags of flour. The drawers for the pots are great.

March 12: The icemaker and the Sub-Zero refrigerator drawers are installed. Nice. I can see down through them, locating missing items.

March 14: Back comes the carpenter to remove the tile from under the dishwasher. We return from a trip to find the backsplash is installed, but the work is sloppy; the icemaker now works; an important plug has decided to die.

March 26: GE sends technicians to fix the microwave and the broken tray on the dishwasher. The backsplash guys will return to remedy their mistakes.

The kitchen is lovely. It has taken a month longer than we had planned, but all the snow certainly didn't help. The best thing we did was to hire the designer and then the contractor. We don't feel that the experience was as horrible as most say.

There's great light in the kitchen now. We can sit at the kitchen table and look out on the garden, the birds, and the dogs playing. *Courtesy of D. Peter Lund.*

Surveys by the real estate industry show that a kitchen is one, if not the most, important feature with potential purchasers. According to a 2003 National Association of Realtors study, a survey of thirty-five United States cities showed that the average kitchen renovation cost is about $69,000, and homeowners recoup approximately 80% during a resale. In some major cities, however, homeowners profited on the renovation.

Architects and Designers

Valerie Lasker, an independent residential designer in San Francisco, owns Altos Design, Inc., which specializes in kitchen and bath design. *Better Homes and Gardens Kitchens and Bath Design* published her work and awarded her first place in the Master Bath Category in 2002. She is an Allied Member of ASID and a member of NKBA.

2451 Filbert St., San Francisco, California 94123
(415) 614-0121
valerie@altosdesign.com

Darnel Aucoin is a registered, state licensed interior designer and president of Darnel Aucoin Interiors, Inc., located in Metarie, Louisiana. Her firm does both residential and commercial design projects, focusing on functional and aesthetically planned spaces. She is a professional member of ASID and is currently the secretary of her local chapter.

449 Betz Place Metairie, Louisiana 70005
(504) 832-5962
darnelaucoin@cox.net

Award-winning designers Paul Engemann, Allied ASID, and Suzanne Barnes, Allied ASID, of Austin-Go-Bostin Interior Designs have been successfully creating wonderful environments for their clients throughout the United States for over a decade. Their client list includes such celebrities as Larry King and Marie Osmond. Their work has been featured on the cover of *Architectural Digest* as well as on national television and HGTV.

372 W. 3800 N. Provo, Utah 84604
(310) 271-6006
(801) 227-0525
info@austingobostin.com
www.austingobostin.com

Victoria Benatar (Urban) is a registered architect (AIA-CAV) and the principal of her own internationally recognized award-winning firm in New York City. She develops architectural, interior design, and digital and urban design projects worldwide. She was an adjunct assistant professor at the Columbia University Graduate School of Architecture, Planning, and Preservation and works as a part-time faculty at Parsons School of Design.

257 E 61 St. #4E New York, New York 10021
(212) 755-0525
vbu@e-arquitectura.com
www.e-arquitectura.com

Tere Bresin's work has been featured in many of New Jersey's prestigious showhouses. Prior to owning Beret Design Group, she was the Director of Design and Senior Designer for several architectural firms. *House Beautiful, Stone World, Design Times,* and several regional magazines have featured her work. She has won many awards for design excellence.

551 Valley Rd., Suite 180 Upper Montclair, New Jersey 07043
(973) 857-4714
Beretdsgn@aol.com

Patricia Davis Brown Fine Cabinetry provides design services to clients with discriminating taste who value innovative design, along with superior craftsmanship and precise attention to detail. The firm's work has been featured in *Traditional Homes Magazine, Southern Accents, Kitchens by Professional Designers, Designer Kitchens and Baths,* and *Vero Home and Design.*

2905 Cardinal Dr. Vero Beach, Florida 32963-1970
(772) 231 1326
PDBFINECAB@aol.com

Cheryl Casey Ross, member of ASID, IIDA, Certified Interior Designer, AIA/SFV Professional Affiliate, has owned Cross Interiors since 1975. A graduate of UCLA in Environmental Art and Interior Design, she is a multi-award winning designer, has been published in over 95 design magazines and books, and participated in 18 design showcase houses. An interior and exterior designer, she specializes in kitchen and bath design.

6712 Colbath Ave., Van Nuys, California 91405
Carpinteria, Balboa Island, Newport Beach
(818) 988-2047
cherylcaseyross@crossinteriors.com
www.crossinteriors.com

Dalia Kitchen Design offers unique home design solutions – from kitchen to bath, from bedroom to family room, and throughout the house. Its design staff unites the customer's aspirations with its unique ability to fulfill them – with experience, distinction, and excellence. The firm provides its customers with the world's finest product lines.

1 Design Center Place Suites 633, 635, 643
Boston Design Center Boston, Massachusetts 02210
(617) 482.2566
info@daliakitchens.com
www.daliakitchendesign.com

Mick De Giulio is a product designer for SieMatic Corporation and a product development consultant for Sub-Zero Freezer/Wolf Appliance companies. In 1995, HGTV asked Mick to help produce its first series on luxury kitchen and bathroom design, and in 2003 *Interior Design* magazine voted him a Kitchen and Bath Design Leader. For 30 years he has created innovative kitchen interiors that have defined the industry. His focus continues to be on creating an enhanced living environment individually suited to each client.

Two Greenwood Sq., Suite 450, 3331 Street Rd., Bensalem, Pennsylvania 19020
(800) 765-5266
(215) 244-6800
siematic@siematic.com
www.siematic.com

Designing spectacular kitchens and baths is a passion for Jennifer Rand, a professional member of ASID and a Certified Kitchen Designer (CKD). She began her career in Manhattan, becoming adept in designing city kitchens. Although the scope and size of her projects have grown, she still enjoys the challenge provided by small urban spaces. Her firm, The Design Company, Ltd., specializes in creative space planning solutions for kitchens, baths, and other residential interiors.

44 Chestnut St. Boston, Massachusetts 02108
(617) 838-3388

Penny Chin's design firm, Elements in Design, is based in San Francisco and Palm Desert, California, and offers a full spectrum of design services, from creation to completion. She believes in working with her clients' to achieve "their wish list while creating an environment that benefits their lifestyle." Best known for her award-winning residential kitchen designs, she has also received awards for her restaurant and hospitality designs. She holds several Design Advisory Board positions for several colleges and has served as president to ASI.

(650) 595-8884
PennyChin@ElementsInDesign.com

Merrie Fredericks, CMKBD, NKBA, and owner of Design Concepts Plus, has won over 22 national awards for design excellence through the NKBA and companies such as Sub-Zero Refrigeration. She has also appeared on HGTV. Numerous national publications have featured her work, and she has acted as a judge for NKBA's national design competition. She has a steadfast commitment to detail and customer satisfaction.

3515 Sawmill Road Newtown Square, Pennsylvania 19073
(610) 355-9485
merriefred@comcast.net

Ria Gulian, ASID, owns Designs by Ria, a New Jersey interior design firm. Her understanding of construction comes from her long and successful working relationships with many area builders. Her renovation projects have earned accolades from clients for her ability to achieve maximum efficiency, storage, and design impact. An NCIDQ-certified designer, she is published in such publications as *House Beautiful, Elegance by Design*, and various New Jersey publications.

51 East Main St., Holmdelm New Jersey 07733
(732) 975-9858
ria@designsbyria.com
www. designsbyria.com

Bruce Goff, ASID, IIDA, NCIDQ, is a principal of Domus Design Group of San Francisco, Reno, and Houston. The firm's philosophy is "Live Better. Work Smarter." Its award-winning designers have worked on homes, offices, hotels, and other institutions for over 25 years. The firm's projects range from kitchen design for private residences to space planning and project management for residences, hotels, and Fortune 500 companies.

120 Thoma St., Reno, Nevada 89501
(775) 323-5608
bruce@domusdesign.com
www.domusdesign.com

Downtown Group Architects, founded in 1984 by partners Peter Wilcox and Mark Winkelman, is named for its "down" sensibility …the lively mix of business, art, passion, and fun that finds its way into their projects. It is best known for its high-end residential work, media facilities, and schools.

236 W. 27th St. Suite 701 New York, New York 10001
(212) 675-9506
www.downtowngroup.com

Laura Trujillo, CKD, ASID joined Dybdahl's Classic Kitchens and Cabinetry 2 years ago, but she brought over 25 years of design experience to the team. Her designs have been published in many consumer and trade magazines and have been featured four times on the cover of *Better Homes and Gardens* magazine. Jill Dybdahl, owner, explores diverse design practices such as Wabi Sabi and Feng Shui. She enjoys helping families create functional "child/elder-friendly" kitchens. The firm's award-winning design team is familiar with current trends as well as classic styles, and they utilize that knowledge to exceed their client's dreams. Dybdahl's Classic Kitchens and Cabinetry has received the following recent awards: Paul Dybdahl, C.K.D. and Nancy Kaiser, C.K.D., 2004 Sub-Zero Design Contest as national and regional winners.

8120 Forsythia St. Middleton, Wisconsin 53562
(608) 831-2500
info@dybkitchens.com

Doreen Fair Westfall, of Eclipse Design Studio, Ltd., is known for her sense of style, keen eye, attention to detail, and ease of communication. With more than 10 years of design experience, Doreen approaches each project individually; her clients have come to expect a quality and timelessness from her interiors that fully meet their needs and exceed their expectations. Doreen specializes in residential design and has participated in the 2003 Junior League of Boston Decorators' Show House.

35 Pinckney Street, Boston, Massachusetts 02114
(617) 877-8803
doreen.westfall@comcast.net

Interdesign Limited's philosophy focuses strongly on the project's natural environment. "Our designs," says Jonathan Isleib," incorporate traditional ideas with contemporary ways of living by drawing on multi-cultural, traditional forms of enduring beauty and adapting them to the client's lifestyle. We strive to achieve a sense of timelessness while creating an exciting sculptural living environment that is in harmony with nature."

101 Shore Road - P.O. Box 250 Old Lyme, Connecticut 06371
(860) 434-8083
email@interdesign-ltd.com

Interior Design Solutions is known for innovative and elegant interiors that stand the test of time – classic, comfortable, and serene. Susan Aiello, ASID, president of Interior Design Solutions, is certified to practice her profession by both the state of New York and the National Council for Interior Design Qualification. She is a professional member of ASID and served as president of the ASID New York Metropolitan Chapter in 1999. She is also a professional affiliate of the New York Chapter of the American Institute of Architects (AIA) and an active member of its Interiors Committee.

300 East 74th St. New York, New York 10021
(212) 628-3938
susan@idsny.com
www.idsny.com

Charlene Keogh, the owner of Keogh Design Inc., has been practicing interior design for 29 years. She has interior design projects throughout the United States and received AIA's Excellence in Interiors award. *Interior Design, Design Times*, and *Dwell* magazines have published her projects. Her work also includes numerous furniture and product designs for individual clients.

180 Duane St. New York, New York 10013
(212) 964-4170
www.keoghdesign.com

Kimball Derrick, CKD, opened The Kitchen Design Studio to showcase his custom cabinet line, K.D. and Steele Cabinetry. His extensive experience in woodworking, architecture, fine arts, and furniture restoration became the predominant skills used when he and partner Joe Steele founded the firm in 1985. Kimball's projects have received numerous regional and national design awards and have been featured in several national publications and books.

10816 Millington Court
Cincinnati OH 45242
(937) 783-2465
(513) 791-1113
info@thekdstudio.com

Cherie Brown of Kitchens by Kleweno has been designing innovative kitchens for 25 years. Whether it is a small city kitchen or a large suburban kitchen, she believes a kitchen should be as functional as it is beautiful. She also believes that it should complement the owner's lifestyle and personality.

4034 Broadway
Kansas City, Missouri 64111
(816) 531-3986
cherie@kleweno.com
www.kleweno.com

Tuulikki Loring's work is characterized by warmth, charm, color, and idiosyncratic choice. In business since 1985, she had designed both contemporary and traditional interiors. Her strength is her Finnish heritage, her use of design and color, and her combinations of antiques with contemporary china and glassware.

33 Bloomfield St., Lexington, Massachusetts 02421
(781) 862-4672
tuulikki@rcn.com

Sydnie Bette Barcenas of LVSB Designs has a degree in interior design and has enjoyed being an interior designer for over four years. She provides independent marketing/consulting/design services on behalf of cabinetmakers, builders, and installers, specializing as a kitchen/bath designer. Her focus is to provide reality to the client's dream design. She is currently Vice-President of Membership for the NKBA Southwest Desert chapter.

(702)328-5040
lvsbdesigns@aol.com

Rupinder Singh, the owner of Mimar Design, is a Boston-based architect with an interest in creating visually clean yet tectonically and materially lavish environments for the residential and commercial client. His design solutions are an integration of aesthetic pleasure, functionality, and durability.

21 Shepard St. #34 Cambridge, Massachusetts 02138
(617) 669-4352
mimardesign@hotmail.com

Nancy Mullan, a professional member of ASID, a certified kitchen designer (CKD), and a licensed home-improvement contractor, has 20 years of experience designing and renovating houses and apartments. Her work has been published in many books and national publications, including the covers of *House Beautiful* and *Country Living*, and she has appeared frequently on TV. A founding member of NKBA's Manhattan Chapter, she has just completed her term as the Chapter Representative to the National Board of Directors. She was ranked among the top design companies in the *Interior Design Magazine* "2003 Kitchen & Bath Design Leader Survey."

204 East 77th St. #1 E New York, New York 10021
(212) 628-4629
info@nancymullan.com

Virginia Smith of Sanders Smith Associates is an award-winning interior designer based in San Francisco. Specializing in residential design with an emphasis on renovation, space planning, and color specification, she is equally comfortable with traditional and contemporary design.

2627 Steiner St. San Francisco, California 9415
(415) 673-3213
sanderss@smith.cnchost.com

Abby Schwartz Associates, Integrated Architecture and Interiors, is a small residential architecture firm with a reputation for high quality customized design, through documentation, and attention to every detail. The firm's spirited pool of talent strives to provide innovative solutions through the simultaneous consideration of both architecture and interior design.

The Woods, 983 Old Eagle School Rd. #610 Wayne, Pennsylvania 19087
(610) 964-9669
avs@icdc.com

Patrick Sutton is the principal of SuttonDesign Interiors LLC. The Virginia-based firm designs and manages large-scale residential renovations, particularly kitchens, living areas, and bathrooms. Sutton's approach, a reaction against standardized and manufactured interiors, emphasizes individualized, handcrafted work carefully tailored to client needs and preferences. The media regularly features his projects throughout the United States.

203 E. Luray Ave. Alexandria, Virginia 22301
(703) 549-5739
www. suttondesign.com

Thielsen Architects, Inc. P.S. is a vibrant design-oriented firm that is committed to creating distinctive environments. It believes that thoughtful spatial organization and sensitivity to the site and natural light achieve sensible design solutions. The firm strives to design architecture that will remain as functional and beautiful over time as it is today.

720 Market St., Suite C Kirkland, Washington 98033
(425) 828-0333
inquiries@thielsen.com
www.thielsenarchitects.com

Key to Acronyms

CMKBD: Certified Master Kitchen and Bath Designer
NKBA: National Kitchen and Bath Association
ASID: American Society of Interior Designers
CKD: Certified Kitchen Designer
NCIDQ: National Council for Interior Design Qualification

Appendix A

Kitchen Design Survey Form

The National Kitchen & Bath Association (NKBA) developed a questionnaire, which is very helpful in designing a kitchen.

General Client Information

1. How long have you lived at, or how much time do you spend at the jobsite residence?_____

2. When was the house built?_____ How old is the present kitchen?_____

3. How did you learn about our firm?_____

4. When would you like to start the project?_____

5. When would you like the project to be completed?_____

6. Has anyone assisted you in preparing a design for the kitchen?_____

7. Do you plan on retaining an interior designer or architect to assist in the kitchen planning?_____

8. Do you have a specific builder/contractor or other subcontractor/specialist with whom you would like to work?_____

9. What portion of the project, if any, will be your responsibility?_____

10. What budget range have you established for your kitchen project?_____

11. How long do you intend to own the jobsite residence?_____

12. What are your plans regarding this home?_____

    a. Is it a long or short-term investment?_____

    b. Is return on investment a primary concern?_____

    c. Do you plan on renting the jobsite residence in the future?_____

13. What family members will share in the final decision-making process?_____

14. Would you like our firm to assist you in securing project financing? _____Yes _____No

15. What do you dislike most about your present kitchen?_____

16. What do you like about your present kitchen?_____

BMFS   1

Specific Kitchen Questions

1. How many household members? (Ask for approximate ages.)
   _____ Adults _____Teens _____Children _____Other
   _____ Pets What types: _____

2. Are you planning on enlarging your family while living here?_____

3. Who is the primary cook?_____
   Is the primary cook left-handed _____ or right-handed _____ ?
   How tall is the primary cook?_____
   Does the primary cook have any physical limitations?_____

4. How many other household members cook?_____
   Who are they?_____
   Do they have a cooking hobby _____ , assist the primary cook with a specific task _____ ,
   or share a menu item with the primary cook?_____
   Is the secondary cook(s) right-handed _____ left-handed _____ ?
   How tall is the secondary cook(s)?_____
   Is a specialized cooking center required for the secondary cook(s)?_____
   Do they have physical limitations? _____

5. How does the family use the kitchen?_____
   _____ Daily Heat & Serve Meals   _____ Daily Full-Course, "From Scratch" Meals
   _____ Weekend Quantity Cooking   _____ Weekend Family Meals
   Other _____

6. Is the kitchen a socializing space?_____

7. How would you like the new kitchen to relate to adjacent rooms?_____

   _____Family Room   _____Dining Room
   _____Family Home Office _____Family TV Viewing

8. What time of day is the kitchen used most frequently?_____

9. What are your kitchen and dining area requests?_____
   _____ Separate Table   _____ 30" Table Height Dining Counter
   _____ New _____ Existing _____ 36" Counter Height
   _____ Size _____ Leaf Extension _____42" Elevated Bar Height Dining Center
   _____ Number of Seated Diners

10. Do you do any specialty cooking? _____ Gourmet _____ Canning _____ Ethnic

11. Do you cook in bulk for freezing _____ and/or leftovers _____ ?

BMFS   2

Page 1   Page 2

Page 3

Specific Kitchen Questions (continued)

12. Do you entertain frequently?_____ Formally _____ Informally

13. Designing the kitchen so that it supports your entertainment style is part of the planning process. Tell me which statement fits you the best:

_____ I like to be the only one in the kitchen with my guests in a separate space that is away from the kitchen

_____ I like to be the only cook in the kitchen, with my guests close by in a family room space that opens onto the kitchen.

_____ I like my guests to be sitting in the kitchen visiting with me while I cook.

_____ I like my guests to help me in the kitchen in meal preparation.

_____ I like my guests to help in the cleanup process after the meal.

_____ I retain caterers who prepare all meals for entertaining.

_____ The caterers come to the home to serve and cleanup.

_____ I stop by the caterers and pick up the food.

_____ I stop at the deli/take-out restaurant to bring part or all of the meal home before entertaining.

The items that I purchase from outside sources are:

_____ Appetizers _____ Salads _____ Soups

_____ Entrees _____ Desserts _____ Other

14. What secondary activities will take place in your kitchen?

_____ Computer _____ Laundry _____ TV/Radio

_____ Eating _____ Planning Desk _____ Wet Bar

_____ Growing Plants _____ Sewing _____ Other

_____ Hobbies _____ Study _____ Other

15. What is your cycle of shopping for food?

_____ Weekly _____ Bi-weekly _____ Daily

16. What types of products/materials do you purchase at the grocery store?

Predominantly fresh food purchased for a specific meal. _____

Predominantly frozen foods purchased for stock. _____

Traditional pantry boxed/packaged/canned goods purchased for stock. _____

(1) Types of canned goods:

_____ Condiments _____ Fruits _____ Soft Drinks _____ Vegetables

(2) Cleaning products stocked in bulk _____

(3) Paper products stocked in bulk _____

(4) Other boxed/packaged food items stocked in bulk _____

(5) Other _____

Page 4

Specific Kitchen Questions (continued)

17. Where do you presently store:

_____ Baking Equipment	_____ Non-Refrigerated Fruits/Vegs.	_____ Spices
_____ Boxed Goods		_____ Table/Appointments
_____ Canned Goods	_____ Paper Products	_____ Linens
_____ Cleaning Supplies	_____ Pet Food	_____ Wrapping Materials
_____ Dishes	_____ Pots & Pans	_____ Leftover Containers
_____ Glassware	_____ Recycle Containers	_____ Other
_____ Laundry/Iron	_____ Serving Trays	_____ Other
_____ Equipment	_____ Specialty Cooking Vessels (Wok, Etc.)	_____ Other

Legend: B = Base Cabinet   C = Countertop   L = Laundry Room
         BA = Basement   AG = Appliance Garage T = Tall Cabinet
         BC = Bookcase   D = Desk   W = Wall Cabinet

18. What type of specialized storage is desired?

_____ Bottle	_____ Dishes	_____ Plastic
_____ Bread Board	_____ Display Items	_____ Soft Drink Cans
_____ Bread Box	_____ Glassware	_____ Spice
_____ Cookbook	_____ Lids	_____ Vegetables
_____ Cutlery	_____ Linen	_____ Wine
_____ Other	_____ Other	_____ Other

19. What type of cabinet interior storage are you interested in?

_____ Lazy Susan	_____ Roll-outs	_____ Drawer Ironing Board
_____ Pantry	_____ Towel Bar	_____ Toe-Kick Step Stool
_____ Vertical Dividers	_____ Tilt-out	_____ Other
_____ Recycling/Waste Bins	_____ Drawer Head	_____ Other

20. What small specialty electrical appliances do you use in your kitchen?

_____ Blender	_____ Elec. Fry Pan	_____ Wok
_____ Can Opener	_____ Food Processor	_____ Other
_____ Crock Pot	_____ Griddle	_____ Other
_____ Coffee Pot	_____ Toaster	_____ Other

21. Have you considered relocating or changing windows or doors in the new plan? _____

22. How do you plan on sorting recyclable trash in your new kitchen?

Sorting into: _____ Plastic   _____ Compact refuse

_____ Paper   _____ Trash

_____ Glass

a._____ clear

b._____ brown

c._____ green

23. Would you like a sorting station in the:

_____ kitchen _____ utility room _____ garage _____ basement _____ outside?

Page 5

Design Information

1. What type of feeling would you like your new kitchen space to have?

Sleek/Contemporary _____	Warm & Cozy Country _____
Traditional _____	Open & Airy _____
Strictly Functional _____	Formal _____
Family Retreat _____	Personal Design Statement _____

2. What colors do you like _____ and dislike _____ ?

3. What colors are you considering for your new kitchen? _____

4. What are color preferences of other family members? _____

5. Have you made a sketch or collected pictures of ideas for your new kitchen? _____

6. Design Notes:

_____

_____

_____

_____

_____

_____

_____

_____

_____

_____

_____

_____

_____

_____

_____

_____

Courtesy of The National Kitchen & Bath Association.

Appendix B

Decisions, Decisions

These days, an infinite array of cooking, washing, and refrigerating appliances from the basic to the amazing are available. Just go to the next home show in your area and be dazzled.

If you love to cook (or refrigerate, for that matter), some may be worth your investment. At the very least, knowing about some new appliances might fire your imagination.

To begin, make a wish list of everything you'd like in the kitchen. Concurrently, begin noticing kitchens and making notes about those you admire. Visit a home improvement center, opening and shutting doors, imagining putting your groceries away, touching and feeling cabinets, countertops, etc. Make a list of those that you like and their costs.

If you plan to undertake the kitchen design on your own, measure your kitchen, including wall space and ceiling height. Make a scale drawing, indicating existing cabinets, light fixtures, windows and doors, outlets, appliances, and plumbing.

Dishwashers

Once upon a time, the dishwasher was considered a luxury appliance; today, we consider it a definite necessity.

American dishwashers differ greatly from their European counterparts. United States dishwashers are geared to clean dishes. European dishwashers, on the other hand, wash the dishes, but, in general, use less water and energy than their domestic counterparts. One way they save energy is by eliminating the food grinder that disposes of the debris on our American plates and replacing it with a filter.

Basically, the low maintenance Unites States versions get the job done, are less expensive, but have higher water and electricity costs. Their sleek European counterparts conserve resources, are more expensive to buy but are cheaper to use.

United States manufacturers have been improving their product to reduce water usage, ensure maximum spray coverage, and enhance insulation for quieter cycles. Just as Americans are finding ways to use less water and energy, so Europeans are making their units less high-maintenance.

Some have combined European design and engineering coupled with American manufacturing. One manufacturer has a line equipped with electronic controls that are "capable of performing hundreds of tasks." One feature allows the consumer to load and wash just the top half of the dishwasher.

Some companies offer a dishwasher in drawer form. Two of the units can be stacked to fit in the space of one conventional dishwasher. Since they can be operated independently, you don't need to ever put your dishes away in a cupboard.

The trend today is towards compact, portable, and limited-release versions. Some manufacturers have models with a third rack for baking sheets and shallow pans or for your cutlery.

Cooktops and Ovens

Fuel choice is a major decision when it comes to buying a stove or a combined cooktop and oven. Most homeowners prefer an electric oven with a gas cooktop because gas burners usually generate more BTUs and electric ovens heat more evenly.

It's difficult to believe that so many people live on take-out when you look at the ranges available today. Let me give you a sampling from just two manufacturers

One possible stove. *Courtesy of Dalia Kitchen Design.*

The two ovens in one manufacturer's double wall oven each have ten heat modes, nine for cooking and one for cleaning. Each heating mode has a purpose such as convection, convection with bottom heat, convection with broiling, top heat, baking stone, and self-clean. Yes, the oven is available with an optional baking stone to simulate brick oven baking of pizzas, breads, and rolls.

The other manufacturer offers vent hoods, rotisseries, pot racks, shelves, wine racks, cabinets, and even cookware to match their ranges. One range has a gas-powered, flat cast-iron, cooking surface that provides graduated heat for making fine gourmet sauces; others have a reversible snack/grille plate, two electric burners or a barbecue grill. They come in a choice of 15 colors and five metal trim colors.

Refrigerators

Refrigerators come in a wide range of styles, colors, and with a variety of features. To decide what you want, you need to make some important decisions about what is important to you, whether it is freezer over or under, number of refrigerator bins, storage of gallon jugs, humidity controlled bins, or ice/water dispenser.

The market is crowded with high-end refrigerators that offer more and

You have to keep a tidy refrigerator if you elect this style. *Courtesy of Dalia Kitchen Design.*

more unusual features. One has a refrigerator with a special bin that promises to chill wine to the perfect temperature in 15 minutes while others have digital temperature readouts, shelves that move up and down at the touch of a lever, removable coolers to deliver the ice to your guests. Then there are the see-through glass doors so you can "showcase your food" like those charming French bistros. But who wants to keep that refrigerator constantly cleaned and what about those partially used salad dressing bottles?

A farmhouse style in the city.
Courtesy of Dalia Kitchen Design.

Drawer refrigerators are becoming more common. Originally, both drawers had to be freezers or refrigerators, now you can choose one of each. One manufacturer offers a variety of specialized models including a wine cooler. All fit in a standard 24" wide undercounter space.

Drinks are on the house with wine chillers or beverage centers – just what every home needs. They can even match your décor with custom sideboards and illuminated interiors.

Sinks

Modern technology makes it easy to enjoy an undermounted sink in a laminate, tiled, or granite counter top. These sleek, easy-to-clean options can be used throughout the home, in the kitchen, bathroom, or laundry. No longer will you have dirt around the rim.

Stainless steel is the most popular type of sink available, but you now need to decide what shape you prefer. Totally baffled, I was pleased when someone told me, "You want a D shape."

You may want a really expensive chrome faucet. Some faucets are actually stainless steel with either matte black or matte blue accents. Faucets can have ceramic cartridges, high-arc spouts, and different spray patterns. A pullout spray version allows you to adjust the water flow from a stream to a spray.

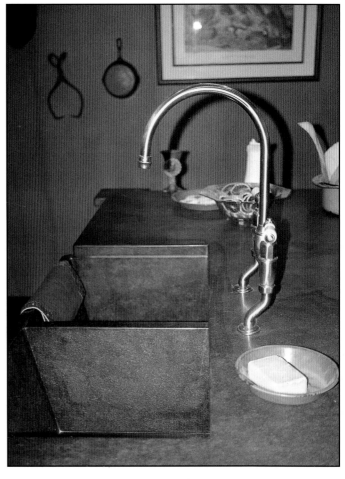

Counter Culture

In reviewing the possible choices, I asked friends and designers for their shopping tips. Some suggestions:

Consider your living style. Are you a chopping board type or do you just cut and peel anywhere? Do you use trivets or just place hot pots anywhere? A new expensive countertop does not necessarily mean you change your living patterns. Even if you do, you may very well regress.

Analyze the total costs, including the costs for resealing and maintenance.

Combine different materials for appearance and function. It is not a decorating dictum that you have granite throughout, for example. You can combine materials, placing less expensive materials where they are not so obvious or where they are used for one particular activity. For example, you could install a butcher block for your baking. Ask your kitchen designer to help you with the mixing and matching.

This counter will stand up well. *Courtesy of Dalia Kitchen Design.*

Think about how your countertop will look in a few years. My tile counter was home for all the bacteria in the neighborhood because of the heavy culinary activity that occurred in my kitchen. It also became quite brown from the spilled coffee. On the other hand, tile can be quite lovely as backsplashes or on counters without much usage.

Use your own common sense. If the material is porous, uneven, or has seams, bacteria and even dirt will probably collect there, waiting to be found by …your mother?

Assess the maintenance of your countertop when you select a particular material. We selected a tile counter, which held up well, but the grout required a dedicated housekeeper. Some materials require replaning of scratches and gouges; other require periodic resealing.

Consider your backsplash and flooring when purchasing your countertop. Do you want the counter to contrast with or match?

Cabinets

Much of a kitchen's style comes from the cabinets. Lighting, flooring, and counter tops have a lesser effect but they can enhance the style.

Today's oak, birch, or natural cherry cabinets lighten up the kitchen. Placing matching wood panels over the appliances makes the room appear larger, although your guests can never find the refrigerator or your trash bin.

Replacing the cabinet hardware is a simple and inexpensive decorative touch. You have a wide range to choose from in hardware and home design stores.

A formal cabinet. *Courtesy of Dalia Kitchen Design.*   And an informal one. *Courtesy of Dalia Kitchen Design.*

Floors

The floor sets the stage for the kitchen and further defines its style. Many people recommend a hardwood floor because it is more resilient, easier on your feet, and can be refinished in a variety of ways. Today's stone floors are meant to be admired so they are simply covered with a transparent sealer to prevent staining.

Lighting

The quality of kitchen lighting makes a major difference in a kitchen. Kitchen lighting, task, ambient, and accent, should consider utility, safety, comfort, and mood. Under cabinet warm fluorescent or halogen lights can add good working light.

Overheads can give you some easy ambient light. If you install a dimmer, you can adjust the light lower for those intimate dinners and brighter for working in the kitchen.

If you replace a solid cabinet door with a glass-paneled one, you can add interior lights, which will add warmth to the room.

Appendix C

Design Professionals
—Susan Aiello, ASID, CID
Interior Design Solutions

Because of all of the technical and procedural challenges involved in designing a city kitchen, it is best to work with a qualified design professional.

There are three types of design professionals that one can use – architects, interior designers, and designers that specialize in kitchens. One way to evaluate the technical competence of such a professional is to find out if he or she is actually certified to practice the profession. Registered Architects, NCIDQ Certified Interior Designers, and Certified Kitchen Designers (CKDs) have all passed stringent nationally administered tests that represent tangible proof of their technical expertise relevant to the kitchen design and implementation process. Each type of profession has its pluses and minuses, as briefly summarized below, and what you may want to do is to use a combination of skills to achieve the best result.

Architects

Architects are usually experts on shape and form. They have a firm grasp of the "big picture," the "envelope" of the kitchen. For projects where the design affects the exterior of the building or involves moving load-bearing walls, an architect's expertise is really essential. Architects are usually highly adept at documenting their designs, as well as the entire construction process, and communicating with contractors.

The disadvantage of working solely with an architect is that he or she might not pay as much attention as an interior designer or a kitchen designer will to the way that you will actually use your kitchen, the inclusion of creature comforts, and the details that can make your kitchen special. Many architects would rather have one perfect spoon than several sets of flatware; consequently, they often have difficulty understanding how much storage a client may need. Architects generally focus on form, rather than finishes, so they are unlikely to want to help you find the tiles, cabinet hardware, etc., that can make your kitchen unique.

Interior Designers

Interior designers are adept at conceptualizing what a room will look like when it has been completed. Certified Interior Designers who have passed the NCIDQ have proven competence in space planning and in interviewing clients to effectively distinguish their wants and needs and to develop designs that address clients' requirements. As a consequence, professional interior designers usually communicate well with clients and are able to translate their clients' personalities into the details, finishes, and colors that help make the client's kitchen individualistic. Since many interior designers are collectors, they often have more dishes, glasses, and serving pieces than most people, so they are generally skilled at optimizing storage space.

The disadvantage of working solely with an interior designer is that he or she may not know as much about structure, mechanics, or building codes as an architect or as much about appliances and certain technical aspects of kitchen design as a CKD does.

Not all interior designers are space planners or have kitchen design experience. Make sure, if you are hiring an interior designer to do renovation work on your kitchen, that he or she has a fair amount of this type of experience. The NCIDQ is the nationally recognized test of professionalism for interior designers and includes fairly extensive sections covering space planning and code compliance. Ask your designer for examples of kitchens that he or she has planned and executed, as part of your due diligence.

Certified Kitchen Designers

CKDs work exclusively on kitchens and nothing else. They are normally quite knowledgeable about the latest developments and trends affecting kitchens, and they can discuss the features and specifications of the most current appliances in more detail than most interior designers and architects can. Not every employee working in a kitchen store has CKD credentials, so it's a good idea to make sure that the person who will be designing your kitchen is, in fact, a certified professional.

The disadvantage of working with CKDs is that they often are not independent but are affiliated with particular stores or showrooms. Accordingly, their designs are usually based on products that their store or showroom sells. Moreover, since they often charge a very modest design fee and make their money based on the cost of what you purchase, there can be a built-in disincentive to save you money. This caveat, of course, does not apply to independent CKDs.

Additionally, CKDs are often less concerned with the overall architectural context of your home than an architect or an interior designer. Therefore, a room designed by this type of professional might not have the same "flow" with the rest of the house as a room designed by one of the other types of design professionals.

Courtesy of Woodruff & Brown Photography.

Project Index